WRIGHT FAMILY
BIRTH, MARRIAGE, PERSONAL PROPERTY TAX AND CENSUS RECORDS

CUMBERLAND COUNTY, VIRGINIA

Robert N. Grant

HERITAGE BOOKS
2015

HERITAGE BOOKS
AN IMPRINT OF HERITAGE BOOKS, INC.

Books, CDs, and more—Worldwide

For our listing of thousands of titles see our website
at
www.HeritageBooks.com

Published 2015 by
HERITAGE BOOKS, INC.
Publishing Division
5810 Ruatan Street
Berwyn Heights, Md. 20740

Copyright © 2015 Robert N. Grant

All rights reserved. No part of this book may be reproduced or transmitted in any form or by any means, electronic or mechanical, including photocopying, recording or by any information storage and retrieval system without written permission from the author, except for the inclusion of brief quotations in a review.

International Standard Book Numbers
Paperbound: 978-0-7884-5602-2
Clothbound: 978-0-7884-6080-7

WRIGHT FAMILY

BIRTH RECORDS 1853 TO 1896

MARRIAGE RECORDS 1748 TO 1900

PERSONAL PROPERTY TAX LISTS 1782 TO 1844

CENSUS RECORDS 1810 Through 1900

CUMBERLAND COUNTY, VIRGINIA

Revised as of October 18, 2014

WRIGHT FAMILY

BIRTH RECORDS

1853 TO 1896

CUMBERLAND COUNTY, VIRGINIA

Revised as of October 18, 2014

© 2014, Robert N. Grant
0954(101814)

Introduction To Appendix: Birth Records, Cumberland County, Virginia

This document is an appendix to a larger work titled Sorting Some Of The Wrights Of Southern Virginia. The work is divided into parts for each family of Wrights that has been researched. Each part is divided into two sections; the first section is text discussing the family and the evidence supporting the relationships and the second section is a descendants chart summarizing the relationships and information known about each individual.

The appendices to the work (of which this document is one) present source records for persons named Wright by county and by type of record with the identification of the person named and their Wright ancestors to the extent known.

The source for the records listed in this appendix is the following:

   1)   Cumberland County, Virginia, Birth Records available from the Clerk of the Circuit Court, P.O. Box 8, Cumberland, Virginia 23040.

The identification of a person or their ancestor by year and county indicates their year of death and county of residence at death. For example, "1763 Thomas Wright of Bedford County" indicates that this was the Thomas Wright who died in 1763 in Bedford County. If no state is listed after the county, the state is Virginia; counties in states other than Virginia will have a state listed after the county, as in "1876 William S. Wright of Highland County, Ohio".

A parenthetical after the name indicates an identification of the person when a place of death is not yet known, as in "John Wright (Goochland County Carpenter)". A county in parentheses after the name indicates the county with which that person was most identified when no evidence of the place of death has yet been found, as in "Grief Wright (Bedford County)".

All or portions of the text and descendants charts for each Wright family identified are available from the author:

   Robert N. Grant
   15 Campo Bello Court   (H) 650-854-0895
   Menlo Park, California 94025   (O) 650-614-3800

This is a work in process and I would be most interested in receiving additional information about any of the persons identified in these records in order to correct any errors or expand on the information given.

0954(101814)

Appendix: Cumberland County, Virginia, Birth Records

Date	Name of Child	Other Information	Identification
1859/10/10	Phillip Wright	Color: White Sex: Male Born: Alive Place: Cumberland County Father's Name: Seymer Wright Father's Occupation: Miller Father's Res: Cumberland County Mother's Name: Catharine Wright Informant: S. Wright Relationship: Father	Phillip Wright, son of Seymour Wright, probably grandson of 1863 William Wright of Buckingham County, probably great grandson of 1803 John Wright of Cumberland County, great great grandson of 1770 John Wright of Cumberland County, and great great great grandson of 1769 George Wright of Essex County
1865/12/00	Catharine Wright	Color: White Sex: Female Born: Alive Place: Cumberland County Condition at Birth: No deformity Father's Name: Seamour A. Wright Father's Occupation: Miller Father's Res: Cumberland County Mother's Name: Catharine Wright Informant: S. A. Wright Relationship: Father	Catherine Wright, daughter of Seymour Wright, probably granddaughter of 1863 William Wright of Buckingham County, probably great granddaughter of 1803 John Wright of Cumberland County, great great granddaughter of 1770 John Wright of Cumberland County, and great great great granddaughter of 1769 George Wright of Essex County
1866/08/00	Cornelias Wright	Status: Slave Sex: Male Born: Alive Place: Cumberland County Condition at Birth: No deformity Father's Name: Wyatt Wright Father's Occupation: Farmer Father's Res: Cumberland County Mother's Name: Agnes Wright Informant: V. Parrish Relationship: Friend	Cornelius Wright, son of Wyatt Wright

Appendix: Cumberland County, Virginia, Birth Records

Date	Name of Child	Other Information	Identification
1867/12/00	Martha Wright	Color: Colored Sex: Female Born: Alive Place: Cumberland County Condition at Birth: No deformity Father's Name: Wyatt Wright Father's Occupation: Laborer Father's Res: Cumberland County Mother's Name: Agnes Wright Informant: N. G. Flippen Relationship: Friend	Martha Wright, daughter of Wyatt Wright
1870/12/00	Anna Wright	Color: Colored Status: Slave Sex: Male(?) Born: Alive Father's Occupation: Farmer Father's Residence: Cumberland County Mother's Name: Agnes Wright	

INDEX

Flippen, N. G., 2
Wright, Agnes, 1, 2
Wright, Anna, 2
Wright, Catharine, 1
Wright, Cornelias, 1
Wright, Martha, 2
Wright, Phillip, 1
Wright, S. A., 1
Wright, Seamour A., 1
Wright, Seymer, 1
Wright, Wyatt, 1, 2

WRIGHT FAMILY

MARRIAGE RECORDS

1748 TO 1900

CUMBERLAND COUNTY, VIRGINIA

Revised as of October 18, 2014

© 2014, Robert N. Grant
0194(101814)

Introduction To Appendix: Marriage Records, Cumberland County, Virginia

This document is an appendix to a larger work titled Sorting Some Of The Wrights Of Southern Virginia. The work is divided into parts for each family of Wrights that has been researched. Each part is divided into two sections; the first section is text discussing the family and the evidence supporting the relationships and the second section is a descendants chart summarizing the relationships and information known about each individual.

The appendices to the work (of which this document is one) present source records for persons named Wright by county and by type of record with the identification of the person named and their Wright ancestors to the extent known.

The sources for the records listed in this appendix are the following:

1) Cumberland County, Virginia, Marriage Records, available from the Clerk of the Circuit Court, P.O. Box 8, Cumberland, Virginia 23840.

2) Marriage Records 1749-1840, Cumberland County, Virginia, compiled by Katharine B. Elliott, South Hill, Virginia, 1969, repriated by Southern Historical Press, Inc., P.O. Box 738, Easley, South Carolina 29641-0738.

The identification of a person or their ancestor by year and county indicates their year of death and county of resence at death. For example, "1763 Thomas Wright of Bedford County" indicates that this was the Thomas Wright who died in 1763 in Bedford County. If no state is listed after the county, the state is Virginia; counties in states other than Virginia will have a state listed after the county, as in "1876 William S. Wright of Highland County, Ohio".

A parenthetical after the name indicates an identification of the person when a place of death is not yet known, as in "John Wright (Goochland County Carpenter)". A county in parentheses after the name indicates the county with which that person was most identified when no evidence of the place of death has yet been found, as in "Grief Wright (Bedford County)".

All or portions of the text and descendants charts for each Wright family identified are available from the author:

Robert N. Grant
15 Campo Bello Court   (H) 650-854-0895
Menlo Park, California 94025   (O) 650-614-3800

This is a work in process and I would be most interested in receiving additional information about any of the persons identified in these records in order to correct any errors or expand on the information given.

0194(101814)

Appendix: Cumberland County, Virginia, Marriages

Book/Page	Date	Marriage Record	Other Information	Identification
	1785/10/30	William Wright & Elisabeth Wade	Husb Res: Cumberland County Wife Res: Cumberland County Surety: Samuel Williams	1838 William Wright of Cumberland County, son of 1774 George Wright of Cumberland County and grandson of 1769 George Wright of Essex County
	1785/12/26	Gabriel Wright & Catharine Ransone	Daughter of Flmsd. Ransone Consent: Flmsd. Ransone Husb Res: Cumberland County Wife Res: Cumberland County Surety: Creed Taylor	1807 Gabriel Wright of Buckingham County, son of 1774 George Wright of Cumberland County and grandson of 1769 George Wright of Essex County
	1788/05/12	Isaac Stephens or Stevens & Mary Wright	Surety: Thomas Wright	Mary (Wright) Stephens, daughter of 1791 Thomas Wright of Cumberland County and granddaughter of 1769 George Wright of Essex County
	1788/07/16	William Glenn & Elizabeth Wright	Husb Res: Cumberland County Wife Res: Cumberland County Surety: Thomas Wright	Elizabeth (Wright) Glenn, daughter of 1791 Thomas Wright of Cumberland County and granddaughter of 1769 George Wright of Essex County
	1788/08/11	Saymer Wright & Frances Williams	Husb Res: Cumberland County Wife Res: Cumberland County Surety: William Wright	1823 Saymer Wright of Cumberland County, son of 1770 John Wright of Cumberland County and grandson of 1769 George Wright of Essex County
	1789/03/27	Charles Carter & Susanna Wright	Daughter of Thomas Wright Husb Res: Cumberland County Wife Res: Cumberland County Surety: Isaac Stephens	Susannah (Wright) Carter, daughter of 1791 Thomas Wright of Cumberland County and granddaughter of 1769 George Wright of Essex County
	1793/03/00	William Wright & Elizabeth Woodson		1838 William Wright of Cumberland County, son of 1774 George Wright of Cumberland County and grandson of 1769 George Wright of Essex County
	1794/01/27	Benjamin Cullin & Sarah Wright	Husb Res: Cumberland County Wife Res: Cumberland County Surety: Samuel Wright	Sarah (Wright) Cullin, daughter of 1791 Thomas Wright of Cumberland County and granddaughter of 1769 George Wright of Essex County

Appendix: Cumberland County, Virginia, Marriages

Book/Page	Date	Marriage Record	Other Information	Identification
	1794/01/27	Samuel Wright & Patience C. Glenn	Husb Res: Cumberland County Wife Res: Cumberland County Surety: William Glenn	1809 Samuel Wright of Laurens County, South Carolina, son of 1791 Thomas Wright of Cumberland County and grandson of 1769 George Wright of Essex County
	1794/09/27	William Ligon & Patsy Wright	Daughter of Elizabeth Wright Consent of Elizabeth Wright Witness: William Wright Witness: P. C. Wright Surety: Saymer Wright	Patsy (Wright) Ligon, daughter of 1791 Thomas Wright of Cumberland County and granddaughter of 1769 George Wright of Essex County
	1806/01/10 or 1807/01/10 or 1808/01/10	Francis Wright & Sally Baily	Husb Res: Cumberland County Wife Res: Cumberland County Surety: Jas. Baily	
	1806/02/18	Allen Wilson & Elizabeth Wright	Daughter of Saymer Wright Witness: Jos. Vaughan Surety: Jesse Michaux	Elizabeth (Wright) Wilson, daughter of 1823 Saymer Wright of Cumberland County, granddaughter of 1770 John Wright of Cumberland County, and great granddaughter of 1769 George Wright of Essex County
	1806/06/17	Drury M. Allen & Sally A. Wright	Daughter of William Wright Consent: William Wright Witness: John A. Allen Witness: Henry Ransone Husb Res: Cumberland County Wife Res: Cumberland County Surety: Henry Woodson	Sally Anderson (Wright) Allen, daughter of 1838 William Wright of Cumberland County, granddaughter of 1774 George Wright of Cumberland County, and great granddaughter of 1769 George Wright of Essex County
	1807/08/24	Joseph Redd & Else Wright	Surety: Richard Michaux	Else (Wright) Redd, daughter of 1805 Benjamin Wright of Cumberland County, granddaughter of 1770 John Wright of Cumberland County, and great granddaughter of 1769 George Wright of Essex County
	1808/06/08	Robert Wright & Elisabeth Clopton	Consent: Elizabeth Clopton Bond: June 5, 1808 Husb Res: Cumberland County Wife Res: Cumberland County Surety: Newton Ford	Possibly Robert Wright, son of 1831 Robert Wright of Smith County, Tennessee

0194(101814)

Appendix: Cumberland County, Virginia, Marriages

Book/Page	Date	Marriage Record	Other Information	Identification
	1808/12/23	Green Wright & Polly A. Burton	Husb Res: Cumberland County Wife Res: Cumberland County Surety: Jno. Nunnally	Nathaniel Green Wright of Smith County, Tennessee, son of 1831 Robert Wright of Smith County, Tennessee
	1811/03/21	Prior Wright & Mary Glover	Daughter of Robert Glover, deceased Surety: William Glover	Pryor Wright, son of John Wright (Bent Creek)
	1811/12/23	Flemsted R. Wright & Sintha Sharp	Consent: Syntha Sharpe Witness: John Christo, Jr. Witness: Charles Presser Husb Res: Cumberland County Wife Res: Cumberland County Surety: Charles Roper	1874 Flemstead R. Wright of Bath County, Kentucky, son of 1807 Gabriel Wright of Buckingham County, grandson of 1774 George Wright of Cumberland County, and great grandson of 1769 George Wright of Essex County
	1813/05/11	Archibald D. Wright & Mary Raine	Husb Res: Cumberland County Wife Res: Cumberland County Surety: Anderson Cocke	1819 Archibald D. Wright of Prince Edward County, son of 1810 Archibald Wright of Buckingham County, grandson of 1774 George Wright of Cumberland County, and great grandson of 1769 George Wright of Essex County
	1815/12/08	George Wright & Sally H. Burton	Consent: N. Ford for his ward Salley Burton Witness: Hez. Ford Witness: Burwell Jeter Husb Res: Cumberland County Wife Res: Cumberland County Surety: Burwell Jeter	George Turner Wright of Smith County, Tennessee, son of 1831 Robert Wright of Smith County, Tennessee
	1817/11/24	John W. Wilson & Martha Wright	Surety: Miller Woodson	Martha (Wright) Wilson, daughter of 1823 Saymer Wright of Cumberland County, granddaughter of 1770 John Wright of Cumberland County, and great granddaughter of 1769 George Wright of Essex County
	1818/10/06	James C. Coleman & Nancy Wright	Surety: Robert Wright	

Appendix: Cumberland County, Virginia, Marriages

Book/Page	Date	Marriage Record	Other Information	Identification
	1818/12/11	John Woodson Wright & Nancy Lancaster	Daughter of John Lancaster Witness: William Lancaster Witness: John M. Woodson Husb Res: Cumberland County Wife Res: Cumberland County Surety: John M. Woodson (Bond not dated, but date on back)	1853 John Woodson Wright of Cumberland County, son of 1838 William Wright of Cumberland County, grandson of 1774 George Wright of Cumberland County, and great grandson of 1769 George Wright of Cumberland County
	1820/05/09	Thomas Wright & Mary Ann Daniel	Daughter of Leonard Daniel Consent: Leonard Daniel Witness: B. J. Savidge Witness: Jesse Jeter Witness: James M. Daniel Husb Res: Cumberland County Wife Res: Cumberland County Surety: James M. Daniel	1852 Thomas H. Wright of Bedford County, son of 1810 John Wright of Bedford County and grandson of 1767 Francis Wright of Amherst County
	1820/11/25	Edward Walton & Martha Wright	Wife Par: Lewis Isbell Surety: Archibald McLaurine	Martha (Isbell) (Wright) Walton, widow of 1819 Archibald D. Wright of Prince Edward County, a son of 1810 Archibald Wright of Buckingham County, grandson of 1774 George Wright of Cumberland County, and great grandson of 1769 George Wright of Essex County
	1830/03/22	William R. Wright & Judith A. B. Mosby	Husb Res: Cumberland County Wife Res: Cumberland County Surety: Miller Woodson	
	1833/07/12	Phineas G. Wright & Mary B. Tatum	Consent: Mary Tatum Surety: Andrew J. Anderson	1844 Phineas Glover Wright of Cumberland County, son of Pryor Wright and grandson of John Wright (Bent Creek)
	1836/07/25	James Wood or Woodson & Sarah S. Wright	Husb Res: Cumberland County Wife Res: Cumberland County Surety: Jno. W. Wilson	Sarah S. (_____) (Wright) Wood, widow of 1835 Phillip W. Wright of Cumberland County, a son of 1823 Saymer Wright of Cumberland County, grandson of 1770 John Wright of Cumberland County, and great grandson of 1769 George Wright of Essex County

0194(101814)

Appendix: Cumberland County, Virginia, Marriages

Book/Page	Date	Marriage Record	Other Information	Identification
	1839/10/15	William D. Price & Mary A. Wright	Oath of James Dejarnett that Mary A. Wright is over 21 Husb Res: Cumberland County Wife Res: Cumberland County Surety: James Dejarnette	
	1842/09/30	William B. Anderson & Mary B. Wright	Daughter of Elijah Glover Witness: Lucian L. Singleton Witness: Miss Martha K. Hudgens Witness: Thomas H. Hudgens Husb Res: Cumberland County Wife Res: Cumberland County Surety: Lucian L. Singleton Minister: Poindexter P. Smith	Mary B. (Glover) (Wright) Anderson
	1845/05/01	Thomas Wright & Sally Ann Green	Husb Res: Cumberland County Wife Res: Cumberland County Surety: Nelson Wright Minister: E. P. Wilson	
	1845/08/26	Pascal J. North & Armetha Wright (Mrs)	Oath of Putnam A. Blackwell that Armetha Wright is a widow Husb Res: Cumberland County Wife Res: Cumberland County Surety: Putnams A. Blackwell	
	1847/01/18	George A. Wright & Eliza F. Penick	Consent of Nathl. Peneck Witness: John P. Wright Witness: Henry(?) J. Tuggle(?) Husb Res: Cumberland County Wife Res: Cumberland County Surety: John P. Wright	1879 George Anderson Wright of Campbell County, son of 1811 John Wright of Campbell County and grandson of Robert Wright, Sr. (Campbell County)

Appendix: Cumberland County, Virginia, Marriages

Book/Page	Date	Marriage Record	Other Information	Identification
	1868/10/31	Robert Wright & Milly Page	Place: Cumberland County Va. Color: coloured Husb Age: 21 Wife Age: 19 Husb Cond: Single Wife Cond: Single Husb Birth: Cumberland County Va Wife Birth: Cumberland County Va Husb Res: Cumberland County Va Wife Res: Cumberland County Va Husb Par: Henry & Sophia Wright (Col) Wife Par: Isham & Amelia Page (col) Occup: Farm Hand	Robert Wright, son of Henry Wright
	1868/12/23	Littleberry A. Huddleston & Sallie A. Wright	Place: Cumberland County Va. Husb Age: 37 years Wife Age: 23 years Husb Cond: Single Wife Cond: Single Husb Birth: Appomattox County, Va Wife Birth: Buckingham County Va Husb Res: Cumberland County Va Wife Res: Cumberland County Va Husb Par: Littlebeerry & Ann Huddleston Wife Par: Seymour & Catharine Wright Occup: Farmer	Martha or Sarah "Sallie" A. (Wright) Huddleston, daughter of 1898 Seymour A. Wright of Amelia County, granddaughter of 1863 William Wright of Buckingham County, probably great granddaughter of 1803 John Wright of Cumberland County, great great granddaughter of 1770 John Wright of Cumberland County, and great great great granddaughter of 1769 George Wright of Essex County

Appendix: Cumberland County, Virginia, Marriages

Book/Page	Date	Marriage Record	Other Information	Identification
	1870/08/21	Edmund Wright & Cary Ann Langhorne	Place: Brown Church, Cumberland County, Va. Color: coloured Husb Age: 22 years Wife Age: 22 years Husb Cond: Single Wife Cond: Single Husb Birth: Cumberland County Va. Wife Birth: Cumberland County Va. Husb Res: Cumberland County Va. Wife Res: Cumberland County Va. Husb Par: Hal: & Sophia Wright (coloured) Wife Par: Albert: & Kereziah Langhorne (coloured) Occup: Farmer	Edmund Wright, son of Hal Wright
	1873/04/19	William S Wright & Molly C. Coleman	Place: Cumberland Color: Colo Husb Age: 26 years Wife Age: 22 years Husb Cond: Single Wife Cond: Single Husb Birth: Amelia Cty Wife Birth: Buckingham Cty Husb Res: Amelia Cty Wife Res: Cumberland Husb Par: Saymer & Catharine Wright Wife Par: G Coleman & Caroline G Coleman Occup: Farm Hand	William S. Wright, son of 1898 Seymore A. Wright of Amelia County, grandson of 1863 William Wright of Buckingham County, probably great grandson of 1803 John Wright of Cumberland County, great great grandson of 1770 John Wright of Cumberland County, and great great great grandson of 1769 George Wright of Essex County

Appendix: Cumberland County, Virginia, Marriages

Book/Page	Date	Marriage Record	Other Information	Identification
	1874/12/24	Jno S. Wright & Virginia E. Scott	Place: Cumberland Color: White Husb Age: 24 years Wife Age: 18 years Husb Cond: Single Wife Cond: Single Husb Birth: Buckingham Wife Birth: Powhatan Husb Res: Cumberland Wife Res: Cumberland Husb Par: Seymour & Catharine Wright Wife Par: Jno A & Mary T Scott Occup: Farmer Minister: No return	John S. Wright, son of 1898 Seymore A. Wright of Amelia County, grandson of 1863 William Wright of Buckingham County, probably great grandson of 1803 John Wright of Cumberland County, great great grandson of 1770 John Wright of Cumberland County, and great great great grandson of 1769 George Wright of Essex County
	1874/06/27	Seymour Wright & Pattie Allen	Place: Cumberland County, Va. Color: coloured Husb Age: 40 years Wife Age: 25 years Husb Cond: Widowed Wife Cond: Widowed Husb Birth: Cumberland County Va. Wife Birth: Cumberland County Va. Husb Res: Cumberland County Va. Wife Res: Cumberland County Va. Husb Par: Ben & Oley Wright (col) Wife Par: Phil. & Ann Alber (col) Occup: Farmer	Seymour Wright, son of Benjamin Wright

0194(101814)

Appendix: Cumberland County, Virginia, Marriages

Book/Page	Date	Marriage Record	Other Information	Identification
	1886/12/23	Jonas Manville Wright & Mattie J. Davis	Place: Caira Cumberland County, Va. Color: White Husb Age: 25 years of age Wife Age: 17 years of age Husb Cond: Single Wife Cond: Single Husb Birth: Buckingham County Wife Birth: Powhatan County Va. Husb Res: Buckingham County Wife Res: Cumberland County Husb Par: James & Elizabeth Wright Wife Par: Benj F & Martha S Davis Occup: Farmer	Jonas Manville Wright, son of 1905 James A. Wright of Buckingham County, grandson of 1863 William Wright of Buckingham County, probably great grandson of 1803 John Wright of Cumberland County, great great grandson of 1770 John Wright of Cumberland County, and great great great grandson of 1769 George Wright of Essex County
	1894/12/19	Thos Jackson Wright & Eva M. Toney	Place: Cumberland Co Va Color, White Husb Age: 25 years Wife Age: 17 years Husb Cond: Single Wife Cond: Single Husb Birth: Buckingham Co Va Wife Birth: Cumberland Co Va Husb Res: Cumberland Co Va Wife Res: Cumberland Co Va Husb Par: James & Elizabeth Wright Wife Par: E B. & Mary Toney Occup: Farmer	Thomas Jackson Wright, son of 1905 James A. Wright of Buckingham County, grandson of 1863 William Wright of Buckingham County, probably great grandson of 1803 John Wright of Cumberland County, great great grandson of 1770 John Wright of Cumberland County, and great great great grandson of 1769 George Wright of Essex County

Appendix: Cumberland County, Virginia, Marriages

Book/Page	Date	Marriage Record	Other Information	Identification
	1895/12/11	Willie T. Wright & Rosa L. Huddleston	Place: Cumberland Co Va Color, White Husb Age: 21 years Wife Age: 22 years Husb Cond: Single Wife Cond: Single Husb Birth: Prince Edward Co Va Wife Birth: Cumberland Co Va Husb Res: Cumberland Co Va Wife Res: Cumberland Co Va Husb Par: L. C. & Sarah Wright Wife Par: Sam & Nannie Huddleston Occup: Farmer	William John Wright, son of Lafayette Clifton Wright, grandson of William P. Wright, great grandson of Daniel P. Wright, great great grandson of 1811 John Wright of Campbell County, and great great great grandson of Robert Wright, Sr. (Campbell County)
	1900/12/26	Henry Wright & Mallie Williamson	Place: Chamblissburg, Bedford County Color: Colored Husb Age: 22 Wife Age: 23 Husb Cond: Single Wife Cond: Single Husb Birth: Bedford County Wife Birth: Bedford County Husb Res: Bedford County Wife Res: Bedford County Husb Par: Jesse & Parthenia Wright Wife Par: Major & Lucinda Williamson Occup: Farming	Henry Wright, son of Jesse Wright

0194(101814)

INDEX

Alber, Ann, 8
Alber, Phil., 8
Allen, Drury M., 2
Allen, John A., 2
Allen, Pattie, 8
Anderson, Andrew J., 4
Anderson, William B., 5
Baily, Jas., 2
Baily, Sally, 2
Blackwell, Putnam A., 5
Burton, Polly A., 3
Burton, Salley, 3
Burton, Sally H., 3
Carter, Charles, 1
Christo Jr., John, 3
Clopton, Elisabeth, 2
Clopton, Elizabeth, 2
Cocke, Anderson, 3
Coleman, Caroline G, 7
Coleman, G, 7
Coleman, James C., 3
Coleman, Molly C., 7
Cullin, Benjamin, 1
Daniel, James M., 4
Daniel, Leonard, 4
Daniel, Mary Ann, 4
Davis, Benj F, 9
Davis, Martha S, 9
Davis, Mattie J., 9
Dejarnett, James, 5
Dejarnette, James, 5
Ford, Hez., 3
Ford, N., 3
Ford, Newton, 2
Glenn, Patience C., 2
Glenn, William, 1, 2
Glover, Elijah, 5
Glover, Mary, 3
Glover, Robert, 3

Glover, William, 3
Green, Sally Ann, 5
Huddleston, Ann, 6
Huddleston, Littlebeerry, 6
Huddleston, Littleberry A., 6
Huddleston, Nannie, 10
Huddleston, Rosa L., 10
Huddleston, Sam, 10
Hudgens, Martha K., 5
Hudgens, Thomas H., 5
Isbell, Lewis, 4
Jeter, Burwell, 3
Jeter, Jesse, 4
Lancaster, Nancy, 4
Lancaster, William, 4
Langhorne, Albert, 7
Langhorne, Cary Ann, 7
Langhorne, Kereziah, 7
McLaurine, Archibald, 4
Michaux, Jesse, 2
Michaux, Richard, 2
Mosby, Judith A. B., 4
North, Pascal J., 5
Nunnally, Jno., 3
Page, Amelia, 6
Page, Isham, 6
Page, Milly, 6
Peneck, Nathl., 5
Penick, Eliza F., 5
Presser, Charles, 3
Price, William D., 5
Raine, Mary, 3
Ransone, Catharine, 1
Ransone, Flmsd., 1
Ransone, Henry, 2
Redd, Joseph, 2
Roper, Charles, 3
Savidge, B. J., 4
Scott, Jno A, 8

Scott, Mary T, 8
Scott, Virginia E., 8
Sharp, Sintha, 3
Sharpe, Syntha, 3
Singleton, Lucian L., 5
Smith, Poindexter P., 5
Stephens, Isaac, 1
Tatum, Mary, 4
Tatum, Mary B., 4
Taylor, Creed, 1
Toney, E B., 9
Toney, Eva M., 9
Toney, Mary, 9
Tuggle(?), Henry(?) J., 5
Vaughan, Jos., 2
Wade, Elisabeth, 1
Walton, Edward, 4
Williams, Frances, 1
Williams, Samuel, 1
Williamson, Lucinda, 10
Williamson, Major, 10
Williamson, Mallie, 10
Wilson, Allen, 2
Wilson, E. P., 5
Wilson, Jno. W., 4
Wilson, John W., 3
Wood, James, 4
Woodson, Elizabeth, 1
Woodson, Henry, 2
Woodson, James, 4
Woodson, John M., 4
Woodson, Miller, 3
Woodson, Miller, 4
Wright, Archibald D., 3
Wright, Armetha, 5
Wright, Ben, 8
Wright, Catharine, 6, 7, 8
Wright, Edmund, 7
Wright, Elizabeth, 1, 2, 9

Wright, Else, 2
Wright, Flemsted R., 3
Wright, Francis, 2
Wright, George, 3
Wright, George A., 5
Wright, Green, 3
Wright, Hal:, 7
Wright, Henry, 6, 10
Wright, James, 9
Wright, Jesse, 10
Wright, Jno S., 8
Wright, John Lancaster, 4
Wright, John P., 5
Wright, John Woodson, 4
Wright, Jonas Manville, 9
Wright, L. C., 10
Wright, Martha, 3, 4
Wright, Mary, 1
Wright, Mary A., 5
Wright, Mary B., 5
Wright, Nancy, 3
Wright, Nelson, 5
Wright, Oley, 8
Wright, P. C., 2
Wright, Parthenia, 10
Wright, Patsy, 2
Wright, Phineas G., 4
Wright, Prior, 3
Wright, Robert, 2, 3, 6
Wright, Sallie A., 6
Wright, Sally A., 2
Wright, Samuel, 1, 2
Wright, Sarah, 1, 10
Wright, Sarah S., 4
Wright, Saymer, 1, 2, 7
Wright, Seymour, 6, 8
Wright, Sophia, 6, 7
Wright, Susanna, 1
Wright, Thomas, 1, 4, 5

Wright, Thos Jackson, 9
Wright, William, 1, 2
Wright, William R., 4
Wright, William S, 7
Wright, Willie T., 10

WRIGHT FAMILY

PERSONAL PROPERTY TAX LISTS

1782 TO 1844

CUMBERLAND COUNTY, VIRGINIA

Revised as of October 22, 2014

© 2014, Robert N. Grant
0884(102214)

Introduction To Appendix: Personal Property Tax Records for Cumberland County, Virginia

This document is an appendix to a larger work titled <u>Sorting Some Of The Wrights Of Southern Virginia</u>. The work is divided into parts for each family of Wrights that has been researched. Each part is divided into two sections; the first section is text discussing the family and the evidence supporting the relationships and the second section is a descendants chart summarizing the relationships and information known about each individual.

The appendices to the work (of which this document is one) present source records for persons named Wright by county and by type of record with the identification of the person named and their Wright ancestors to the extent known.

The source for the records listed in this appendix is the following:

1) Cumberland County, Virginia, Personal Property Tax Lists, available from the Virginia State Library & Archives, 11th & Capitol Streets, Richmond, Virginia 23219.

The identification of a person or their ancestor by year and county indicates their year of death and county of residence at death. For example, "1763 Thomas Wright of Bedford County" indicates that this was the Thomas Wright who died in 1763 in Bedford County. If no state is listed after the county, the state is Virginia; counties in states other than Virginia will have a state listed after the county, as in "1876 William S. Wright of Highland County, Ohio".

A parenthetical after the name indicates an identification of the person when a place of death is not yet known, as in "John Wright (Goochland County Carpenter)". A county in parentheses after the name indicates the county with which that person was most identified when no evidence of the place of death has yet been found, as in "Grief Wright (Bedford County)".

All or portions of the text and descendants charts for each Wright family identified are available from the author:

Robert N. Grant
15 Campo Bello Court   (H) 650-854-0895
Menlo Park, California 94025   (O) 650-614-3800

This is a work in process and I would be most interested in receiving additional information about any of the persons identified in these records in order to correct any errors or expand on the information given.

0884(102214)

1782 PERSONAL PROPERTY TAX LIST

CUMBERLAND COUNTY, VIRGINIA

Appendix: Cumberland County, Virginia, 1782 Personal Property Tax List:

Proprietors Names	No. free Tithables	No. Slaves	No. Horses	No. Cattle	No. Wheels	No. Ordinary licenses	Amount Tax	Identification
Thomas Wright	1	15	7	35			£9.2.9	1791 Thomas Wright of Cumberland County, son of 1769 George Wright of Essex County
William Wright	1	1	2	7			1.5.9	1838 William Wright of Cumberland County, son of 1774 George Wright of Cumberland County and grandson of 1769 George Wright of Essex County
Seymore Wright	1	7	6	14			4.15.6	1823 Saymer Wright of Cumberland County, son of 1770 John Wright of Cumberland County and grandson of 1769 George Wright of Essex County
Griffin Wright	1	8	4	15			5.1.6	1816 Griffin Wright of Franklin County, North Carolina, son of 1769 George Wright of Essex County
George Wright	1	9	6	18			5.16.6	1790 George Wright of Cumberland County, son of 1774 George Wright of Cumberland County and grandson of 1769 George Wright of Essex County
Henry Wright	1	9	10	18		1	11.4.6	1795 Henry Wright of Camden County, Georgia, son of 1774 George Wright of Cumberland County and grandson of 1769 George Wright of Essex County
John Wright	2	4	1	17			3.6.3	1803 John Wright of Cumberland County, son of 1770 John Wright of Cumberland County and grandson of 1769 George Wright of Essex County
Archer Wright	1	1	1				1.2.0	1810 Archibald Wright of Buckingham County, son of 1774 George Wright of Cumberland County and grandson of 1769 George Wright of Essex County

1783 PERSONAL PROPERTY TAX LIST

CUMBERLAND COUNTY, VIRGINIA

Appendix: Cumberland County, Virginia, 1783 Personal Property Tax List:

List A:

Whom Chargeable	Names of taxable persons	No. covering horses and price of season	No. ordinary licenses	No. Wheels	No. free tithe-ables above 21 years	No. slaves above 18 years	No. slaves under 18 years	No. horses except covering horses
Thomas Wright	himself 1 - Ceasar, Ben, Pompey, Hannah Jane Hannah, C_ Moses, Rachel, Harry, George, Adam, Aggy, Joe Silva, Humphrey, John, Haney, Lucy, 12				1	6	12	7
Seymore Wright	himself 1 - Jack, Jude, Copper, 3 - Dinah, Jack, Jesse, Lucy, Will, Jude, 6				1	3	6	8
William Wright	himself 1 - Ralph, 1				1		1	3
George Wright	himself 1 - James, Sam, Dinah, 3 - Wills, Amey, Joy, Daniel 4				1	3	4	7
John Wright	himself, John Griggs, 2 Jim, Harry, 2 - Cloe, York, 2				2	2	2	1

0884(102214)

Appendix: Cumberland County, Virginia, 1783 Personal Property Tax List:

Whom Chargeable [Continued from prior page]	Cattle	Amount Tax	Identification
Thomas Wright	29	10.11.3	1791 Thomas Wright of Cumberland County, son of 1769 George Wright of Essex County
Seymore Wright	13	5.19.3	1823 Saymer Wright of Cumberland County, son of 1770 John Wright of Cumberland County and grandson of 1769 George Wright of Essex County
William Wright	7	1. 7.9	1838 William Wright of Cumberland County, son of 1774 George Wright of Cumberland County and grandson of 1769 George Wright of Essex County
George Wright	17	4.18.3	1790 George Wright of Cumberland County, son of 1774 George Wright of Cumberland County and grandson of 1769 George Wright of Essex County
John Wright	13	3. 5.3	1803 John Wright of Cumberland County, son of 1770 John Wright of Cumberland County and grandson of 1769 George Wright of Essex County

Appendix: Cumberland County, Virginia, 1783 Personal Property Tax List:

List B:

Whom chargeable	No. Covering horses and price of Season	No. ordinary licenses	No. Wheels	No. free persons	No. slaves above 16 years	No. slaves under 16 years	No. horses except coverg horses	No. cattle	Amount tax	Identification
Thomas Wright				1	6	12	7	29	10.11.3	1791 Thomas Wright of Cumberland County, son of 1769 George Wright of Essex County
Seymore Wright				1	3	6	8	13	5.19.3	1823 Saymer Wright of Cumberland County, son of 1770 John Wright of Cumberland County and grandson of 1769 George Wright of Essex County
William Wright				1		1	3	7	1. 7.9	1838 William Wright of Cumberland County, son of 1774 George Wright of Cumberland County and grandson of 1769 George Wright of Essex County
George Wright				1	3	4	7	17	4.16.3	1790 George Wright of Cumberland County, son of 1774 George Wright of Cumberland County and grandson of 1769 George Wright of Essex County
John Wright				2	2	2	1	13	3. 5.3	1803 John Wright of Cumberland County, son of 1770 John Wright of Cumberland County and grandson of 1769 George Wright of Essex County

0884(102214)

1784 PERSONAL PROPERTY TAX LIST

CUMBERLAND COUNTY, VIRGINIA

Appendix: Cumberland County, Virginia, 1784 Personal Property Tax List:

Whom chargeable	No. Covering Horses & prices of season	No. Ordy. licences	No. Wheels	No. free tiths. above 21 years	No. Negroes tiths.	No. Negroes not tiths.	No. Horses except Cov: Horses	No. Cattle	Amount Tax	Identification
Thomas Wright				1	6	11	8	27	10. 2.9	1791 Thomas Wright of Cumberland County, son of 1769 George Wright of Essex County
John Wright				2	2	3	3	9	3.18.3	1803 John Wright of Cumberland County, son of 1770 John Wright of Cumberland County and grandson of 1769 George Wright of Essex County
George Wright				1	3	4	6	18	4.16.6	1790 George Wright of Cumberland County, son of 1774 George Wright of Cumberland County and grandson of 1769 George Wright of Essex County
Seymer Wright				1	4	6	5	12	6. 3.0	1823 Saymer Wright of Cumberland County, son of 1770 John Wright of Cumberland County and grandson of 1769 George Wright of Essex County
William Wright				1		1	4	7	1. 9.9	1838 William Wright of Cumberland County, son of 1774 George Wright of Cumberland County and grandson of 1769 George Wright of Essex County

Appendix: Cumberland County, Virginia, 1784 Personal Property Tax List:

Whom chargeable	No. Covering Horses & prices of season	No. Ordy. licences	No. Wheels	No. free tiths. above 21 years	No. Negroes tiths.	No. Negroes not tiths.	No. Horses except Cov: Horses	No. Cattle	Amount Tax	Identification
Archer Wright				1	5	4	9	10	6. 0.6	1810 Archibald Wright of Buckingham County, son of 1774 George Wright of Cumberland County and grandson of 1769 George Wright of Essex County

10.

1785 PERSONAL PROPERTY TAX LIST

CUMBERLAND COUNTY, VIRGINIA

Appendix: Cumberland County, Virginia, 1785 Personal Property Tax List:

Whom chargeable	No. Cov. Horses and price of season	No. Ord: Licences	No. Wheels	No. free tithables	No. negro Tithables	No. Young Negroes	No. Horses excd. Cov: Horses	No. Cattle	Amount Tax.	Amt. Cert.	Identification
Gabriel Wright				0			1		12.0		1807 Gabriel Wright of Buckingham County, son of 1774 George Wright of Cumberland County and grandson of 1769 George Wright of Essex County
William Wright				1			3	3	16.9		1838 William Wright of Cumberland County, son of 1774 George Wright of Cumberland County and grandson of 1769 George Wright of Essex County
Saymore Wright				1	4	8	6	14	7.5.6		1823 Saymer Wright of Cumberland County, son of 1770 John Wright of Cumberland County and grandson of 1769 George Wright of Essex County
Archibald Wright		1		1	6	5	6	8	11.14		1810 Archibald Wright of Buckingham County, son of 1774 George Wright of Cumberland County and grandson of 1769 George Wright of Essex County
John Wright				2	2	3	4	8	4.0.0		1803 John Wright of Cumberland County, son of 1770 John Wright of Cumberland County and grandson of 1769 George Wright of Essex County
Thomas Wright				1	6	13	8	23	11.1.9		1791 Thomas Wright of Cumberland County, son of 1769 George Wright of Essex County

0884(102214)

Appendix: Cumberland County, Virginia, 1785 Personal Property Tax List:

Whom chargeable	No. Cov. Horses and price of season	No. Ord: Licences	No. Wheels	No. free tithables	No. negro Tithables	No. Young Negroes	No. Horses excd. Cov: Horses	No. Cattle	Amount Tax.	Amt. Cert.	Identification
George Wright				1	3	4	7	13	4.17.3		1790 George Wright of Cumberland County, son of 1774 George Wright of Cumberland County and grandson of 1769 George Wright of Essex County

0884(102214)

13.

1786 PERSONAL PROPERTY TAX LIST

CUMBERLAND COUNTY, VIRGINIA

Appendix: Cumberland County, Virginia, 1786 Personal Property Tax List:

Whom chargeable	No. covering horses and price of the season	Ordinary Licences	Wheels of riding car-riages	Free tythes	Negro Tythes	Negroes not Tythes	Horses except cover-ing horses	Cattle	Specie Tax	Identification
John Wright				2	3	2	4	17		1803 John Wright of Cumberland County, son of 1770 John Wright of Cumberland County and grandson of 1769 George Wright of Essex County
Archibald Wright				1	6	7	5	11		1810 Archibald Wright of Buckingham County, son of 1774 George Wright of Cumberland County and grandson of 1769 George Wright of Essex County
Saymore Wright				1	4	6	6	15		1823 Saymer Wright of Cumberland County, son of 1770 John Wright of Cumberland County and grandson of 1769 George Wright of Essex County
Thomas Wright				2	6	14	9	24		1791 Thomas Wright of Cumberland County, son of 1769 George Wright of Essex County
Jacob Wright				1	1	1	2	2		

0884(102214)

1787 PERSONAL PROPERTY TAX LIST

CUMBERLAND COUNTY, VIRGINIA

Appendix: Cumberland County, Virginia, 1787 Personal Property Tax List:

Date Receiving list from Individuals 1787	names of Persons Chargeable with Tax	names of white Male tithables above 21	Number of white Males above 16 under 21	Blacks above 16	Blacks under 16	horses &c	Cattle	Carriage wheels	ordinary licenses	Billard Tables	Stud horses
March 17	Jacob Wright	Jacob Wright			2	3	2				
March 30	George Wright	himself & James Love		3	4	6	19				
March 24	Archibald Wright	Archibald Wright		6	7	4	13				
March 10	Saymore Wright	Saymore Wright	1	4	9	5	20				
April 2	Thomas Wright	himself & James Wright		7	15	7	34				
March 30	John Wright	himself & John Griggs		3	3	4	13				

0884(102214)

Appendix: Cumberland County, Virginia, 1787 Personal Property Tax List:

names of Persons Chargeable with Tax [Continued from prior page]	Rates Covering	Physicians	apothecaries	Surgeons	Spacie	Certificates	Identification
Jacob Wright							
George Wright							1790 George Wright of Cumberland County, son of 1774 George Wright of Cumberland County and grandson of 1769 George Wright of Essex County
Archibald Wright							1810 Archibald Wright of Buckingham County, son of 1774 George Wright of Cumberland County and grandson of 1769 George Wright of Essex County
Saymore Wright							1823 Saymer Wright of Cumberland County, son of 1770 John Wright of Cumberland County and grandson of 1769 George Wright of Essex County
Thomas Wright							1791 Thomas Wright of Cumberland County, son of 1769 George Wright of Essex County
John Wright							1803 John Wright of Cumberland County, son of 1770 John Wright of Cumberland County and grandson of 1769 George Wright of Essex County

20.

1788 PERSONAL PROPERTY TAX LIST

CUMBERLAND COUNTY, VIRGINIA

Appendix: Cumberland County, Virginia, 1788 Personal Property Tax List:

List A:

Date 1788	Names of Persons Chargeable with Tax	White Male Tithes above 16	Total	Blacks above 16	Blacks above 12 and under 16	Horses &c	Carri-age Wheels	Ordinary licences	Billiard Tables	Stud Horses	Price of the Season
Apr 12	Jacob Wright	Jacob Wright	1	1		1					
Apr 21	Paul Wright	Paul Wright	1		0						

0884(102214)

Appendix: Cumberland County, Virginia, 1788 Personal Property Tax List:

Names of Persons Chargeable with Tax [Continued from prior page]	Physicians	Apothecaries	Surgeons		Identification
Jacob Wright					
Paul Wright					

0884(102214)

Appendix: Cumberland County, Virginia, 1788 Personal Property Tax List:

List B:

date Receiving lists from Individuals	persons Names Chargeable with the Tax	Number of Blacks above 12	Horses &c	Car-riage Wheels	Billiard Tables	Stud Horses	Rates cover-ing	Physi-cians	Apothe-caries	Surgeons	Identification
March 15th	John Wright	6	5								1803 John Wright of Cumberland County, son of 1770 John Wright of Cumberland County and grandson of 1769 George Wright of Essex County
March 15th	Saymore Wright	5	5								1823 Saymer Wright of Cumberland County, son of 1770 John Wright of Cumberland County and grandson of 1769 George Wright of Essex County
April 19th	Archibald Wright	4	2								1810 Archibald Wright of Buckingham County, son of 1774 George Wright of Cumberland County and grandson of 1769 George Wright of Essex County
April 15th	Thomas Wright	9	6								1791 Thomas Wright of Cumberland County, son of 1769 George Wright of Essex County

0884(102214)

Appendix: Cumberland County, Virginia, 1788 Personal Property Tax List:

List B:

date Receiving lists from Individuals	persons Names Chargeable with the Tax	Number of Blacks above 12	Horses &c	Carriage Wheels	Billiard Tables	Stud Horses	Rates covering	Physicians	Apothecaries	Surgeons	Identification
April 21th	George Wright	6	5								1790 George Wright of Cumberland County, son of 1774 George Wright of Cumberland County and grandson of 1769 George Wright of Essex County

26.

1789 PERSONAL PROPERTY TAX LIST

CUMBERLAND COUNTY, VIRGINIA

Appendix: Cumberland County, Virginia, 1789 Personal Property Tax List:

List A:

Date 1789	Names of persons Chargeable With Tax	White Male Tithes	Total	Blacks above 16	Total	Blacks above 12 & under 16	Total	horses	Carriage Wheels	Ordinary Licence	Billiard Tables	Stud Horses
May 7	Jacob Wright	Jacob Wright	1					1				
May 6		Paul Wright	1									

0884(102214)

Appendix: Cumberland County, Virginia, 1789 Personal Property Tax List:

Names of Persons Chargeable with Tax [Continued from prior page]	price of the season	phy:	Aps	Surg.	Identification
Jacob Wright					
Paul Wright					

Appendix: Cumberland County, Virginia, 1789 Personal Property Tax List:

List B:

Date Receiving lists from Individuals	persons Names chargeable with the Tax	Number of blacks above 12	Horses &c	Carriage Whl	ordinary licenses	Billiard Tables	Stud Horses	Rate coverg	physicians	apothecaries
March 14th	William Wright	3	3							
April 29th	Saymore Wright	7	5							
April 9th	Thomas Wright	8	4							
May 5th	George Wright	7	6							
April 2d	Archibald Wright	4	2							
April 5th	John Wright	5	5							

0884(102214)

Appendix: Cumberland County, Virginia, 1789 Personal Property Tax List:

List B:

persons Names charge-
able with the Tax
[Continued from
prior page]   Surgeons   Identification

Name	Surgeons	Identification
William Wright		1838 William Wright of Cumberland County, son of 1774 George Wright of Cumberland County and grandson of 1769 George Wright of Essex County
Saymore Wright		1823 Saymer Wright of Cumberland County, son of 1770 John Wright of Cumberland County and grandson of 1769 George Wright of Essex County
Thomas Wright		1791 Thomas Wright of Cumberland County, son of 1769 George Wright of Essex County
George Wright		1790 George Wright of Cumberland County, son of 1774 George Wright of Cumberland County and grandson of 1769 George Wright of Essex County
Archibald Wright		1810 Archibald Wright of Buckingham County, son of 1774 George Wright of Cumberland County and grandson of 1769 George Wright of Essex County
John Wright		1803 John Wright of Cumberland County, son of 1770 John Wright of Cumberland County and grandson of 1769 George Wright of Essex County

0884(102214)

1790 PERSONAL PROPERTY TAX LIST

CUMBERLAND COUNTY, VIRGINIA

Appendix: Cumberland County, Virginia, 1790 Personal Property Tax List:

List A:

Date 1790	Names of Persons Chargeable With Tax	White Male Tithes	Total	Blacks above 16	Total	Blacks above 12 & under 16	Total	horses	Carri-age Wheels	Ordinary Licences	billiard Tables	Stud horses

[No Wrights listed]

0884(102214)

Appendix: Cumberland County, Virginia, 1790 Personal Property Tax List:

Names of Persons
Chargeable with Tax
[Continued from   Price
prior page]   Season   Phy: Ap: Surg: Identification

[No Wrights listed]

Appendix: Cumberland County, Virginia, 1790 Personal Property Tax List:

List B:

date of Receiving lists from Individuals	Persons Names chargeable with the tax	Number of blacks above 16	Number of blacks under 16 but above 12	Horses &c	Car-riage wheels	ordinary licenses	Billiard Table	Stud horses	Rate cover-ing	physi-cians	apothe-caries
April 22th	Thomas Wright	7		5							
April 21th	Mary Wright	6	3	5							
March 31th	John Wright	3	2	5							
April 3d	William Wright	3		2							
May 4th	Saymore Wright	5	4	6							

0884(102214)

Appendix: Cumberland County, Virginia, 1790 Personal Property Tax List:

List B:

Persons Names chargeable with the tax [Continued from prior page]	Surgeons	Identification
Thomas Wright		1791 Thomas Wright of Cumberland County, son of 1769 George Wright of Essex County
Mary Wright		Mary (Wright) (Wright) Williams, daughter of 1770 John Wright of Cumberland County and granddaughter of 1769 George Wright of Essex County and widow of 1790 George Wright of Cumberland County, a son of 1774 George Wright of Cumberland County and grandson of 1769 George Wright of Essex County
John Wright		1803 John Wright of Cumberland County, son of 1770 John Wright of Cumberland County and grandson of 1769 George Wright of Essex County
William Wright		1838 William Wright of Cumberland County, son of 1774 George Wright of Cumberland County and grandson of 1769 George Wright of Essex County
Saymore Wright		1823 Saymer Wright of Cumberland County, son of 1770 John Wright of Cumberland County and grandson of 1769 George Wright of Essex County

38.

1791 PERSONAL PROPERTY TAX LIST

CUMBERLAND COUNTY, VIRGINIA

Appendix: Cumberland County, Virginia, 1791 Personal Property Tax List:

List A:

Date 1791	Names of Persons Chargable with Tax	White Male Tithes	Total	Blacks above 16	Total	Blacks above 12 & under 16	Total	Horses	Carri-age Wheels	Ordinary Licences	Billiard Tables	Stud Horses
	Paul Wright	1										
	Jacob Wright	1										

Appendix: Cumberland County, Virginia, 1791 Personal Property Tax List:

Names of Persons Chargeable with Tax [Continued from prior page]	Price of Season	Identification
Paul Wright		
Jacob Wright		

Appendix: Cumberland County, Virginia, 1791 Personal Property Tax List:

List B:

date Rceving lists from Individuals	Persons Names Chargable with the tax	No. Blacks over 16	No. Blacks under 16 above 12	Horses &c	Car-riage wheels	Ordinary licenses	B Tables	Stud horses	Rates C.	Identification
March 23d	William Wright	3	1	2						1838 William Wright of Cumberland County, son of 1774 George Wright of Cumberland County and grandson of 1769 George Wright of Essex County
March 18th	Thomas Wrights Est	8		7						Estate of 1791 Thomas Wright of Cumberland County, son of 1769 George Wright of Essex County
April 6th	John Wright	5		4						1803 John Wright of Cumberland County, son of 1770 John Wright of Cumberland County and grandson of 1769 George Wright of Essex County
May 4th	Saymore Wright	2	3	3						1823 Saymer Wright of Cumberland County, son of 1770 John Wright of Cumberland County and grandson of 1769 George Wright of Essex County
May 17th	Benjamin Wright	3	2	5						1805 Benjamin Wright of Cumberland County, son of 1770 John Wright of Cumberland County and grandson of 1769 George Wright of Essex County

0884(102214)

1792 PERSONAL PROPERTY TAX LIST

CUMBERLAND COUNTY, VIRGINIA

Appendix: Cumberland County, Virginia, 1792 Personal Property Tax List:

List A:

Date 1792	Names of persons Chargable with Tax	White male Tythes	Total Blacks above 16	Total Blacks above 12 & under 16	Total	Horses	Carri-age wheels	Ordinary Licences	Bllard Tables	Stud Horses	price Season	Identification
June 24	Paul Wright	Paul Wright	1									
June 24	Jacob Wright	Jacob Wright	1									

0884(102214)

Appendix: Cumberland County, Virginia, 1792 Personal Property Tax List:

List B:

date Receiving lists from Individuals	Persons Names Chargable with the tax	Number Blacks over 16	Number of backs under 16 over 12	Horses &c	Car-riage Wheels	Ordinary licenses	Billiard T___	Stud horses	Rates C.	Identification
March 31th	William Wright	3	1	2						1838 William Wright of Cumberland County, son of 1774 George Wright of Cumberland County and grandson of 1769 George Wright of Essex County
April 28th	John Wright	4		6						1803 John Wright of Cumberland County, son of 1770 John Wright of Cumberland County and grandson of 1769 George Wright of Essex County
April 9th	Elizabeth Wright	8		6						Elizabeth (McGehee) Wright, widow of 1791 Thomas Wright of Cumberland County, a son of 1769 George Wright of Essex County
May 7th	Saymore Wright	2	3	3						1823 Saymer Wright of Cumberland County, son of 1770 John Wright of Cumberland County and grandson of 1769 George Wright of Essex County
May 7th	Benjamin Wright	3	2	4						1805 Benjamin Wright of Cumberland County, son of 1770 John Wright of Cumberland County and grandson of 1769 George Wright of Essex County

46.

1793 PERSONAL PROPERTY TAX LIST

CUMBERLAND COUNTY, VIRGINIA

Appendix: Cumberland County, Virginia, 1793 Personal Property Tax List:

List A:

Date of Lists	Names of persons Charged with tax	No. Free Male Tythes	No. Blacks Above 16	No. Blacks Above 12 & under 16	Horses	Carri-age Wheels	Ordy Licence	Billiard Tables	Stud Horses	Price the Season	Identification

[No Wrights listed]

0884(102214)

Appendix: Cumberland County, Virginia, 1793 Personal Property Tax List:

List B:

date receiving lists from Individuals	Persons Names Chargeable with the tax	Number of Blacks above 16	Number of blacks under 16 above 12	Horses &c	Carriage wheels	ordinary L	Billard T	Stud horses	Rates C.	Identification
1793 March 20th	William Wright	2	1	4						1838 William Wright of Cumberland County, son of 1774 George Wright of Cumberland County and grandson of 1769 George Wright of Essex County
April 3d	Thomas Wrights Est	8	1	7						Estate of 1791 Thomas Wright of Cumberland County, son of 1769 George Wright of Essex County
April 19th	Benjamin Wright	3	1	5						1805 Benjamin Wright of Cumberland County, son of 1770 John Wright of Cumberland County and grandson of 1769 George Wright of Essex County
April 19th	Saymore Wright	3	2	4						1823 Saymer Wright of Cumberland County, son of 1770 John Wright of Cumberland County and grandson of 1769 George Wright of Essex County
May 7th	John Wright	5		6						1803 John Wright of Cumberland County, son of 1770 John Wright of Cumberland County and grandson of 1769 George Wright of Essex County

50.

1794 PERSONAL PROPERTY TAX LIST

CUMBERLAND COUNTY, VIRGINIA

Appendix: Cumberland County, Virginia, 1794 Personal Property Tax List:

List A:

Date 1794	Names of persons Charged with Tax	Blacks Above 16	Total	Blacks Above 16 and under 16	Total	Horses	Carri- age Wheels	Ordinary Licences	Billiard Tables	Stud Horses	Price Season	Identification

[No Wrights listed]

Appendix: Cumberland County, Virginia, 1794 Personal Property Tax List:

List B:

date Receiving lists from Individuals	Persons Names Chargeable with the tax	Number of Blacks above 16	Number of Blacks under 16 & over 12	Horses &c	Carriage Ws.	Ordinary L.	Billard T.	Stud horses	Rates C.	Identification
March 20th	Benjamin Wright	3	2	6						1805 Benjamin Wright of Cumberland County, son of 1770 John Wright of Cumberland County and grandson of 1769 George Wright of Essex County
March 20th	Saymore Wright	4	1	5						1823 Saymer Wright of Cumberland County, son of 1770 John Wright of Cumberland County and grandson of 1769 George Wright of Essex County
March 19th	John Wright	5		4						1803 John Wright of Cumberland County, son of 1770 John Wright of Cumberland County and grandson of 1769 George Wright of Essex County
March 29th	William Wright	2	1	3						1838 William Wright of Cumberland County, son of 1774 George Wright of Cumberland County and grandson of 1769 George Wright of Essex County
April 3d	Thomas Wrights Est	9	4	7						Estate of 1791 Thomas Wright of Cumberland County, son of 1769 George Wright of Essex County

54.

1795 PERSONAL PROPERTY TAX LIST

CUMBERLAND COUNTY, VIRGINIA

Appendix: Cumberland County, Virginia, 1795 Personal Property Tax List:

date receiving Lists from Individuals	Persons Names Chargeable with the tax	Number blacks above 16	Number blacks under 16 but above 12	Horses &c	Car- riage Wheels	Ordinary Licences	Billard T.	Stud horses	Rates C.	Identification
March 13th	John Wright	5		6						1803 John Wright of Cumberland County, son of 1770 John Wright of Cumberland County and grandson of 1769 George Wright of Essex County
May 9th	William Wright	2	1	4						1838 William Wright of Cumberland County, son of 1774 George Wright of Cumberland County and grandson of 1769 George Wright of Essex County
May 14th	Elizabeth Wright	7	4	8						Elizabeth (McGehee) Wright, widow of 1791 Thomas Wright of Cumberland County, a son of 1769 George Wright of Essex County
June 11th	Saymore Wright	5		5						1823 Saymer Wright of Cumberland County, son of 1770 John Wright of Cumberland County and grandson of 1769 George Wright of Essex County
June 11th	Benjamin Wright	5	2	7						1805 Benjamin Wright of Cumberland County, son of 1770 John Wright of Cumberland County and grandson of 1769 George Wright of Essex County

0884(102214)

1796 PERSONAL PROPERTY TAX LIST

CUMBERLAND COUNTY, VIRGINIA

Appendix: Cumberland County, Virginia, 1796 Personal Property Tax List:

date receiving lists from Individuals	persons Names Chargeable with the tax	Number of Blacks above 16	Number of Blacks between 12 and 16	Horses &c	Car- riage Wheels	Ordinary licences	Billiard T.	Stud horses	Rates C.	Identification
april 4th	John Wright	5		6						1803 John Wright of Cumberland County, son of 1770 John Wright of Cumberland County and grandson of 1769 George Wright of Essex County
april 5th	Elizabeth Wright	7	5	7						Elizabeth (McGehee) Wright, widow of 1791 Thomas Wright of Cumberland County, a son of 1769 George Wright of Essex County
May 19th	Saymore Wright	5	1	5						1823 Saymer Wright of Cumberland County, son of 1770 John Wright of Cumberland County and grandson of 1769 George Wright of Essex County
May 19th	Benjamin Wright	5	2	6						1805 Benjamin Wright of Cumberland County, son of 1770 John Wright of Cumberland County and grandson of 1769 George Wright of Essex County
May 31th	William Wright	3	1	4						1838 William Wright of Cumberland County, son of 1774 George Wright of Cumberland County and grandson of 1769 George Wright of Essex County

1797 PERSONAL PROPERTY TAX LIST

CUMBERLAND COUNTY, VIRGINIA

Appendix: Cumberland County, Virginia, 1797 Personal Property Tax List:

date receiving lists from Individuals	persons Names chargeable with the tax	Number of blacks over 16	Number of blacks between 12 & 16	Horses &c	Car-riage wheels	Ordinary licences	Billiard T.	Stud horses	Rates C.	Identification
March 14th	John Wright	5		5						1803 John Wright of Cumberland County, son of 1770 John Wright of Cumberland County and grandson of 1769 George Wright of Essex County
March 14th	Saymore Wright	5	1	6						1823 Saymer Wright of Cumberland County, son of 1770 John Wright of Cumberland County and grandson of 1769 George Wright of Essex County
March 14th	Benjamin Wright	7	2	5						1805 Benjamin Wright of Cumberland County, son of 1770 John Wright of Cumberland County and grandson of 1769 George Wright of Essex County
april 10th	Elizabeth Wright	2	1	1						Elizabeth (McGehee) Wright, widow of 1791 Thomas Wright of Cumberland County, a son of 1769 George Wright of Essex County
april 10th	Samuel Wright	6	3	7						1809 Samuel Wright of Laurens County, South Carolina, son of 1791 Thomas Wright of Cumberland County and grandson of 1769 George Wright of Essex County
June 6th	William Wright	4	1	5						1838 William Wright of Cumberland County, son of 1774 George Wright of Cumberland County and grandson of 1769 George Wright of Essex County

0884(102214)

1798 PERSONAL PROPERTY TAX LIST

CUMBERLAND COUNTY, VIRGINIA

Appendix: Cumberland County, Virginia, 1798 Personal Property Tax List:

date receiving lists from Individuals	persons Names Chargeable with the tax	Number of Blacks above 16	Number of Blacks between 12 & 16	Horses &c	Car- riage wheels	Ordin- ary L.	Stud horses	Rates C.	amt. Dollars	amt. Cents	Identification
March 23d	John Wright	5		5					2	20	1803 John Wright of Cumberland County, son of 1770 John Wright of Cumberland County and grandson of 1769 George Wright of Essex County
april 14th	Samuel Wright	3	3	2					2	28	1809 Samuel Wright of Laurens County, South Carolina, son of 1791 Thomas Wright of Cumberland County and grandson of 1769 George Wright of Essex County
april 21th	Elizabeth Wright	4	4	5					3	25	Elizabeth (McGehee) Wright, widow of 1791 Thomas Wright of Cumberland County, a son of 1769 George Wright of Essex County
June 8th	Saymore Wright	5	2	5					2	90	1823 Saymer Wright of Cumberland County, son of 1770 John Wright of Cumberland County and grandson of 1769 George Wright of Essex County
June 8th	Benjamin Wright	7	2	4					3	51	1805 Benjamin Wright of Cumberland County, son of 1770 John Wright of Cumberland County and grandson of 1769 George Wright of Essex County
June 11th	William Wright	3	3	5					2	55	1838 William Wright of Cumberland County, son of 1774 George Wright of Cumberland County and grandson of 1769 George Wright of Essex County

1799 PERSONAL PROPERTY TAX LIST

CUMBERLAND COUNTY, VIRGINIA

Appendix: Cumberland County, Virginia, 1799 Personal Property Tax List:

date receiving lists from Individuals	Names of persons Chargeable with the tax	Number of blacks above 16	Number of blacks between 12 & 16	Horses &c	Car- riage W.	Ordin- ary L.	Stud horses	Rates C.	Dollars Cents	Identification
april 13th	Samuel Wright	7(?)	1	3					2.56	1809 Samuel Wright of Laurens County, South Carolina, son of 1791 Thomas Wright of Cumberland County and grandson of 1769 George Wright of Essex County
april 13th	Elizabeth Wright	6	3	4					3.56	Elizabeth (McGehee) Wright, widow of 1791 Thomas Wright of Cumberland County, a son of 1769 George Wright of Essex County
May 6th	Saymore Wright	5	2	8					4.04	1823 Saymer Wright of Cumberland County, son of 1770 John Wright of Cumberland County and grandson of 1769 George Wright of Essex County
May 6th	Benjamin Wright	7	1	7					4.36	1805 Benjamin Wright of Cumberland County, son of 1770 John Wright of Cumberland County and grandson of 1769 George Wright of Essex County
May 23d	John Wright	5		4					2.68	1803 John Wright of Cumberland County, son of 1770 John Wright of Cumberland County and grandson of 1769 George Wright of Essex County
June 6th	William Wright	4	2	5					3.24	1838 William Wright of Cumberland County, son of 1774 George Wright of Cumberland County and grandson of 1769 George Wright of Essex County

0884(102214)

1800 PERSONAL PROPERTY TAX LIST

CUMBERLAND COUNTY, VIRGINIA

Appendix: Cumberland County, Virginia, 1800 Personal Property Tax List:

date receiving lists from Individuals	persons Names Chargeable with the tax	No. of blacks of over 16	No. of blacks between 12 & 16	horses &c	Car-riage Wheels	Ordinary licences	Stud horses	Rates C.	Dollars Cents	Identification
March 18	Saymore Wright	5	3	8					4.48	1823 Saymer Wright of Cumberland County, son of 1770 John Wright of Cumberland County and grandson of 1769 George Wright of Essex County
March 18	Benjamin Wright	8	2	6					5.12	1805 Benjamin Wright of Cumberland County, son of 1770 John Wright of Cumberland County and grandson of 1769 George Wright of Essex County
April 1th	Samuel Wright	4	1	5					2.80	1809 Samuel Wright of Laurens County, South Carolina, son of 1791 Thomas Wright of Cumberland County and grandson of 1769 George Wright of Essex County
april 12	Elizabeth Wright	6	2	3					3.88	Elizabeth (McGehee) Wright, widow of 1791 Thomas Wright of Cumberland County, a son of 1769 George Wright of Essex County
april 23	William Wright	4	2	5					3.24	1838 William Wright of Cumberland County, son of 1774 George Wright of Cumberland County and grandson of 1769 George Wright of Essex County
June 9	John Wright	6	1	4					3.56	1803 John Wright of Cumberland County, son of 1770 John Wright of Cumberland County and grandson of 1769 George Wright of Essex County

1801 PERSONAL PROPERTY TAX LIST

CUMBERLAND COUNTY, VIRGINIA

Appendix: Cumberland County, Virginia, 1801 Personal Property Tax List:

date receiving lists from Individuals	Persons Names Chargeable With the tax	No. blacks above 16	No. blacks between 12 & 16	horses &c	Car-riage Wheels	Ordinary licences	Stud horses	Rates C.	Dollars Cents	Identification
March 21	Samuel Wright	10	3	9					6.80	1809 Samuel Wright of Laurens County, South Carolina, son of 1791 Thomas Wright of Cumberland County and grandson of 1769 George Wright of Essex County
april 13	Saymore Wright	5	3	9					4.60	1823 Saymer Wright of Cumberland County, son of 1770 John Wright of Cumberland County and grandson of 1769 George Wright of Essex County
april 13	Benjamin Wright	9	2	9			1	12	29.92	1805 Benjamin Wright of Cumberland County, son of 1770 John Wright of Cumberland County and grandson of 1769 George Wright of Essex County
april 18	William Wright	4	2	5					3.24	1838 William Wright of Cumberland County, son of 1774 George Wright of Cumberland County and grandson of 1769 George Wright of Essex County
June 10	John Wright	5	1	5					3.24	1803 John Wright of Cumberland County, son of 1770 John Wright of Cumberland County and grandson of 1769 George Wright of Essex County

0884(102214)

1802 PERSONAL PROPERTY TAX LIST

CUMBERLAND COUNTY, VIRGINIA

Appendix: Cumberland County, Virginia, 1802 Personal Property Tax List:

date Recving lists from Individuals	Persons Names Chargeable With the tax	No. of Blacks above 16	No. of Blacks between 12 & 16	Horses &c	Car- riage W	Ordinary L	Stud horses	Rates C.	Dollars Cents	Identification
March 10	Benjamin Wright	9	3	8			1	10	26.24	1805 Benjamin Wright of Cumberland County, son of 1770 John Wright of Cumberland County and grandson of 1769 George Wright of Essex County
March 12	Saymore Wright	6	2	10					4.72	1823 Saymer Wright of Cumberland County, son of 1770 John Wright of Cumberland County and grandson of 1769 George Wright of Essex County
april 10	Samuel Wright	13	3	8					8.86	1809 Samuel Wright of Laurens County, South Carolina, son of 1791 Thomas Wright of Cumberland County and grandson of 1769 George Wright of Essex County
June 2	William Wright	5	1	6					3.36	1838 William Wright of Cumberland County, son of 1774 George Wright of Cumberland County and grandson of 1769 George Wright of Essex County
June 2	John Wright	6	1	7					3.92	1803 John Wright of Cumberland County, son of 1770 John Wright of Cumberland County and grandson of 1769 George Wright of Essex County

1803 PERSONAL PROPERTY TAX LIST

CUMBERLAND COUNTY, VIRGINIA

Appendix: Cumberland County, Virginia, 1803 Personal Property Tax List:

date recving lists from Individuals	persons Names chargeable with the tax	No. of Blacks over 16	No. of Blacks between 12 & 16	Horses &c	Car-riage Wheels	Ordinary licensess	Stud horses	Rates C.	Dollars Cents	Identification
March 18	Samuel Wright	12	3	8					7.56	1809 Samuel Wright of Laurens County, South Carolina, son of 1791 Thomas Wright of Cumberland County and grandson of 1769 George Wright of Essex County
May 24	Benjamin Wright	9	3	9			1	8	22.36	1805 Benjamin Wright of Cumberland County, son of 1770 John Wright of Cumberland County and grandson of 1769 George Wright of Essex County
May 24	William Wright	5	1	5					3.24	1838 William Wright of Cumberland County, son of 1774 George Wright of Cumberland County and grandson of 1769 George Wright of Essex County
May 24	Saymore Wright	7		10					4.28	1823 Saymer Wright of Cumberland County, son of 1770 John Wright of Cumberland County and grandson of 1769 George Wright of Essex County
May 22	Nancy Wright	5	1	8					3.60	Nancy (_____) (Wright) Dodson, widow of 1803 John Wright of Cumberland County, a son of 1770 John Wright of Cumberland County and grandson of 1769 George Wright of Essex County

0884(102214)

1804 PERSONAL PROPERTY TAX LIST

CUMBERLAND COUNTY, VIRGINIA

Appendix: Cumberland County, Virginia, 1804 Personal Property Tax List:

date recvg Lists from Individuals	Persons Names Chargeable with the Tax	Names of free male Tithables above 16	Blacks Above 16	Total	Blacks between 12 and 16	Total	Horses	Car- riage Wheels	Ordinary Licenses	Stud horses	Rates C
April 14	Saymer Wright	Saymor Wright Charles Robinson Saymer Wright jr	Gabe, jasper, Cesar, Dick Lewis Dinah & Nell	7	Will	1	8				
April 14	Nancy Wright	Burton Anglia John Griggs John Wright	Jim, Harry, Chloe, york Jesse Sallie & Judah	7			9				
July 3	Benjn Wright	Benjn Wright	judah Lum, jack Jesse, Billy, juggie(?), Amy, Sook	9	phillis Bolding & jerry	3	10				
July 4	Wm Wright	Wm Wright	Sibinah, Crissy Judith Jenny, Will & Ned	6			4				

0884(102214)

Appendix: Cumberland County, Virginia, 1804 Personal Property Tax List:

Persons Names Chargeable with the Tax [continued from prior page]	Dollars Cents	Identification
Saymer Wright	4.48	1823 Saymer Wright of Cumberland County, son of 1770 John Wright of Cumberland County and grandson of 1769 George Wright of Essex County
Nancy Wright	4.16	Nancy (____) (Wright) Dodson, widow of 1803 John Wright of Cumberland County, a son of 1770 John Wright of Cumberland County and grandson of 1769 George Wright of Essex County
Benjn Wright	6.48	1805 Benjamin Wright of Cumberland County, son of 1770 John Wright of Cumberland County and grandson of 1769 George Wright of Essex County
Wm Wright	3.12	1838 William Wright of Cumberland County, son of 1774 George Wright of Cumberland County and grandson of 1769 George Wright of Essex County

76.

1805 PERSONAL PROPERTY TAX LIST

CUMBERLAND COUNTY, VIRGINIA

Appendix: Cumberland County, Virginia, 1805 Personal Property Tax List:

John Baughan District:

Date Receiving list	Persons names Chargeable with the tax	free male tith- ables	Blacks Over 16	Blacks over 12	Horses	Car- riage Wheels	Ordinary licenses	Stud horses	Rates C.	Dollars Cents	Identification

[No Wrights listed]

Appendix: Cumberland County, Virginia, 1805 Personal Property Tax List:

List B:

Dates Receiving Lists	Persons names Chargeable with the tax	Free male tithables	Blacks over 16	Blacks over 12	Horses	Carriage Wheels	ordinary Licenses	Stud Horses	rates covering	Dollars Cents	Identification
April 13	Saml. Wright	1		1						.44	1809 Samuel Wright of Laurens County, South Carolina, son of 1791 Thomas Wright of Cumberland County and grandson of 1769 George Wright of Essex County
April 13	Wm Wright	1	5		6					2.92	1838 William Wright of Cumberland County, son of 1774 George Wright of Cumberland County and grandson of 1769 George Wright of Essex County
June 3	Benj. Wrights Est	1	9	2	6					5.56	Estate of 1805 Benjamin Wright of Cumberland County, son of 1770 John Wright of Cumberland County and grandson of 1769 George Wright of Essex County
June 3	Seaymour Wright	2	7	2	7					4.00	1823 Saymer Wright of Cumberland County, son of 1770 John Wright of Cumberland County and grandson of 1769 George Wright of Essex County

1806 PERSONAL PROPERTY TAX LIST

CUMBERLAND COUNTY, VIRGINIA

Appendix: Cumberland County, Virginia, 1806 Personal Property Tax List:

John Baughan District:

Date Receivg list from Individuals	Persons Names Chargeable with the Tax	free male Tyth- ables	Blacks over 16	Blacks between 12 & 16	Horses	C. Wheels	O Licenses	S horses	R: C.	dollars Cents	Identification
May 21	Coleman Wright	1									
June 23	Frs Wright	1									

0884(102214)

Appendix: Cumberland County, Virginia, 1806 Personal Property Tax List:

List B:

Dates Rec R. lists	Persons Names Chd. with Tax	Names of free tithes over 16	Blacks over 16	Blacks over 12	Horses	Carg wheels	S Horses	Rates of Covering	ordinary Licences	Dollars Cents	Identification
Apl 20	Benj. Wrights Est		11	2	7					6.56	Estate of 1805 Benjamin Wright of Cumberland County, son of 1770 John Wright of Cumberland County and grandson of 1769 George Wright of Essex County
Apl 20	Seaymour Wright	Saml Wright Geog Ransone	6	4	7					5.24	1823 Saymer Wright of Cumberland County, son of 1770 John Wright of Cumberland County and grandson of 1769 George Wright of Essex County

1807 PERSONAL PROPERTY TAX LIST

CUMBERLAND COUNTY, VIRGINIA

Appendix: Cumberland County, Virginia, 1807 Personal Property Tax List:

John Baughan District:

Date Receiving list from Individuals	Persons names Chargeable with the tax	free male tyth-ables	Blacks over 16	Blacks between 12 & 16	Horses	C Wheels	Ordinary	S horses	R C	Dollars Cents	Identification
May 25	Frank Wright	1									
May 25	Coleman Wright	1									

0884(102214)

Appendix: Cumberland County, Virginia, 1807 Personal Property Tax List:

Thomas Hobson District:

date Recevg List from Individuals	Persons names Charged with the Tax	free tithes	Blacks over 16	Blacks over 12	Horses	C Wheels	Ordinary	Stud horses	R C	$ tax Cents tax	Identification
	Saymore Wright	3	6	2	7					4.36	1823 Saymer Wright of Cumberland County, son of 1770 John Wright of Cumberland County and grandson of 1769 George Wright of Essex County
	Wm Wright	1	4	1	4					2.68	1838 William Wright of Cumberland County, son of 1774 George Wright of Cumberland County and grandson of 1769 George Wright of Essex County
	Ben Wrights Es		11	1	8					6.24	Estate of 1805 Benjamin Wright of Cumberland County, son of 1770 John Wright of Cumberland County and grandson of 1769 George Wright of Essex County

1809 PERSONAL PROPERTY TAX LIST

CUMBERLAND COUNTY, VIRGINIA

Appendix: Cumberland County, Virginia, 1809 Personal Property Tax List:

John Baughan District:

Date Receiving list from Individuals	Persons Names Chargable With the tax	free male tyth- ables	Blacks over 16	Blacks Between	Horses	C wheels	O licenses	S horses	Rates Cover- ing	$ tax Cts tax	Identification

[No Wrights listed]

0884(102214)

Appendix: Cumberland County, Virginia, 1809 Personal Property Tax List:

List B:

Date receiving lists	Persons Names Chargd with tax	Free tythes	Blacks over 16	Blacks over 12	Horses	Carriage Wheels	Ordinary licence	Stud Horses	Rates covering	Dollars Cents	Identification
	Seaymor Wright	2	6	2	3					4.48	1823 Saymer Wright of Cumberland County, son of 1770 John Wright of Cumberland County and grandson of 1769 George Wright of Essex County
	Green Wright	1	1	1	2					1.72	Nathaniel Green Wright of Smith County, Tennessee, son of 1831 Robert Wright of Smith County, Tennessee
	William Wright	1	3	2	4					2.68	1823 Saymer Wright of Cumberland County, son of 1770 John Wright of Cumberland County and grandson of 1769 George Wright of Essex County

1810 PERSONAL PROPERTY TAX LIST

CUMBERLAND COUNTY, VIRGINIA

Appendix: Cumberland County, Virginia, 1810 Personal Property Tax List:

List A:

Date Receiving list from Individuals	Persons Names Chargable with the tax	free male tyth- ables	Blacks Over 16	Blacks Between	Horses	C Wheels	S horses	R C	fishing license	Tax $ Tax Cts	Identification

[No Wrights listed]

Appendix: Cumberland County, Virginia, 1810 Personal Property Tax List:

List B:

Date receiving lists	Persons Names Charged with tax	free tythes	Blacks over 16	Blacks over 12	Horses	Carriage Wheels	Ordinary licence	Stud Horses	Rates of Covr	Dollars Cts	Identification
	Green Wright	1	3	1	2					2.00	Nathaniel Green Wright of Smith County Tennessee, son of 1831 Robert Wright of Smith County, Tennessee
	Saymor Wright	1	5	2	6					3.80	1823 Saymer Wright of Cumberland County, son of 1770 John Wright of Cumberland County and grandson of 1769 George Wright of Essex County
	William Wright	1	4	1	5					2.80	1838 William Wright of Cumberland County, son of 1774 George Wright of Cumberland County and grandson of 1769 George Wright of Essex County

1811 PERSONAL PROPERTY TAX LIST

CUMBERLAND COUNTY, VIRGINIA

Appendix: Cumberland County, Virginia, 1811 Personal Property Tax List:

List A:

Date Recing list from Individuals	Persons names Chargable with the tax	free tyth- ables over 16	Blacks over 16	Blacks Between 12 & 16	Horses	C Wheels	S horses	R Covg	fishing licens	$ tax Ct tax	Identification

[No Wrights listed]

Appendix: Cumberland County, Virginia, 1811 Personal Property Tax List:

List B:

Persons Charged With tax	Free tithes	Blacks over 16	Blacks over 12	Horses	Carriage Wheels	Ordinary Licence	Stud Horses	Rates Covrg	Dollars Cents	Identification
Saymor Wright	3	5	3	7					4.26	1823 Saymer Wright of Cumberland County, son of 1770 John Wright of Cumberland County and grandson of 1769 George Wright of Essex County

100.

1812 PERSONAL PROPERTY TAX LIST

CUMBERLAND COUNTY, VIRGINIA

Appendix: Cumberland County, Virginia, 1812 Personal Property Tax List:

John Baughan District:

Date Recing list from Individuals	Persons Names Chargable with the tax	free tyth- ables above 16	Blacks above 16	Blacks Between 12 & 16	Horses	Carriage Wheels	Stud horses	R Cov- ering	fishing License	tax $ Cents tax	Identification

[No Wrights listed]

Appendix: Cumberland County, Virginia, 1812 Personal Property Tax List:

List B:

Dates Receiving lists	Persons Names Charged with tax	free tythes	Blacks over 16	Blacks over 12	Horses	Carriage Wheels	Ordn. licence	Stud Horses	Rates Covering	Dollars Cents	Identification
Apl 25	Saymor Wright	2	7	3	7					5.24	1823 Saymer Wright of Cumberland County, son of 1770 John Wright of Cumberland County and grandson of 1769 George Wright of Essex County
Apl 25	Wm Wright	2	5	_(?)						1.11	1838 William Wright of Cumberland County, son of 1774 George Wright of Cumberland County and grandson of 1769 George Wright of Essex County

1813 PERSONAL PROPERTY TAX LIST

CUMBERLAND COUNTY, VIRGINIA

Appendix: Cumberland County, Virginia, 1813 Personal Property Tax List:

John Baughan District:

Date receiving lists from Individuals	Persons Names Chargable with the tax	free white tyth-ables	free persons of colour	Blacks above 16	Blacks between 12 & 16	Horses	Carri-ages	Valu-ation	Stud Horses	Rates Cover-ing	Value of __ __ Griss mill	rent or Value	Tan yards

[No Wrights listed]

0884(102214)

Appendix: Cumberland County, Virginia, 1813 Personal Property Tax List:

John Baughan District:

Persons Names Chargable with the tax [continued from prior page]	Yearly rent	fishing Licens	Tax $ Cents	Identification

[No Wrights listed]

Appendix: Cumberland County, Virginia, 1813 Personal Property Tax List:

Thomas Hobson District:

Persons Names Chd. with Tax	Free tythes	Blacks over 16	Blacks over 12	Horses	Carriage wheels	Ordn. licence	Stud Horses	Rates	Dollars Cents	Identification
Wm Wright	2	5		4					3.59	1838 William Wright of Cumberland County, son of 1774 George Wright of Cumberland County and grandson of 1769 George Wright of Essex County
Saml Wright	1									
Saymor Wright	2	8	2	7					7.02	1823 Saymer Wright of Cumberland County, son of 1770 John Wright of Cumberland County and grandson of 1769 George Wright of Essex County
Jos. Red for Eliza Wright		5	1	5					4.34	Elizabeth (Wright) Redd, daughter of 1805 Benjamin Wright of Cumberland County, granddaughter of 1770 John Wright of Cumberland County, and great granddaughter of 1769 George Wright of Essex County

0884(102214)

1814 PERSONAL PROPERTY TAX LIST

CUMBERLAND COUNTY, VIRGINIA

Appendix: Cumberland County, Virginia, 1814 Personal Property Tax List:

John Baughan District:

Date receivg list from Individuals	Persons Names Chargable with The tax	free white Tythe- ables	free Male Persons of Colour	Blacks Above 16	Blacks Between 12 & 16	Horses	Carri- ages with harness	Valu- ation	Stud horses	rates Cover- ing	Manufac- turing and grist mill	Amount rent or value	Tan yards

[No Wrights listed]

Appendix: Cumberland County, Virginia, 1814 Personal Property Tax List:

John Baughan District:

Persons Names Chargable with The tax [continued from prior page]	Yearly rent	fishing Licens	No Dogs	$ Tax Cts tax	Identification

[No Wrights listed]

Appendix: Cumberland County, Virginia, 1814 Personal Property Tax List:

List B:

Date receivg list from Individuals	Persons names Chargable with the tax	free white tyth-ables	free male persons of colour	Blacks over 16	Blacks between 12 & 16	Horses	Carriage	Valua-tion	Stud horses	Rates Covering	Manufactur-ing Grist & Saw Mills	Amount Rent or Value	Tan yards	yearly rent
	Saymour Wright	2		9	1	8								
	Wm Wright	1		5	1	5								
	Jno W Wright	1												

Appendix: Cumberland County, Virginia, 1814 Personal Property Tax List:

List B:

Persons names Chargable with the tax [Continued from prior page]	Dogs	$ tax Cts tax	Identification
Saymour Wright		9.58	1823 Saymer Wright of Cumberland County, son of 1770 John Wright of Cumberland County and grandson of 1769 George Wright of Essex County
Wm Wright		5.79	1838 William Wright of Cumberland County, son of 1774 George Wright of Cumberland County and grandson of 1769 George Wright of Essex County
Jno W Wright			1853 John Woodson Wright of Cumberland County, son of 1838 William Wright of Cumberland County, grandson of 1774 George Wright of Cumberland County, and great grandson of 1769 George Wright of Essex County

1815 PERSONAL PROPERTY TAX LIST

CUMBERLAND COUNTY, VIRGINIA

Appendix: Cumberland County, Virginia, 1815 Personal Property Tax List:

List A:

Date receivg list from Individuals	Persons names Chargd. with the tax	No of white maills above 16 years old	Above 16 years old	Slaves Between 12 & 16 years old	Between 9 & 12 years old	Horses Asses Mules Mares & Colts	Stud Horse Number	Rates Cover-ing Mares	No of head cattle	2 Wheel Riding Car-riages	Carriages Phaetons & stage wagons	Public Stages	All other 4 wheel Car-riages

[No Wrights listed]

Appendix: Cumberland County, Virginia, 1815 Personal Property Tax List:

List A:

Persons names Chargd. with the tax [continued from prior page	Mills	Toll bridges & ferries	Tan yards	free Male negroes above 16 years old	Watches gilt silver pinch back	Watches Single cast gold	Watches Double cast gold	livery stables & No of stalls or space sufficient for the accomodation of of one horse	Houses in the Country exceeding in value $500	Tee Houses for private use	Tee Houses from which tee is sold	Clocks clocks of wood without Case	Clocks Clocks of wood with Case

[No Wrights listed]

0884(102214)

117.

Appendix: Cumberland County, Virginia, 1815 Personal Property Tax List:

List A:

	Clocks [Cont'd]			printers	Furniture	
				& the	Business secratary or book Case Chest of drawers wardrobe	
	Portraits pictures					
Persons names				Anuel	or Clothe press Dining tables or separate parts there off	prints or Engrav-
Chargd. with	Clocks	of value		sub-	Bedsteads side boards without drawers or doors Tea or Card	ings Mirror or
the tax	princi-	between		scribers	tables in whole or in part Mahogany Celerel or side board	looking Glasses
[continued from	ply of	50 &	Coal	to their	with drawers or doors settee or sofa Chaires Carpets window	piano fortes harpsi-
prior page	Mettle	100$	Pits	papers	curtain or Venetial blinds within the window of any house	chord harp or organ

[No Wrights listed]

Appendix: Cumberland County, Virginia, 1815 Personal Property Tax List:

List A:

Persons names Chargd. with the tax [continued from prior page	Furniture [cont'd]		Dogs	Total amt of tax $ Cts	Identification
	Bureau Secretaries or book case Chest of drawers wardrobe Clothes press of any other wood than Mahogany	urn coffee or tea pot candle stick lamp Chandeliers epergne or grandole decanter pitcher bowl or goblet wash bason stand or Salver Tankard Cup or waiter			

[No Wrights listed]

Appendix: Cumberland County, Virginia, 1815 Personal Property Tax List:

Thomas Hobson District:

Date receivg list from Individuals	Persons names Chargd. with the tax	No of white males above 16 years	Slaves			Horses Asses Mules Mares & Colts	Stud Horses		No. of head of Cattle	Carriages				All other 4 wheel Carriages
			Above 16 years old	Between 12 & 16	Between 9 & 12		No.	Rates Covering Mares		2 Wheel Riding Carriages	Phaetons & Stage Waggons	Publick Stages		
	Philip Wright	1				2								
	Wm Wright	1	8		2	6			19					
	Jno W Wright	1												
	Saymor Wright Jr	1				1								

0884(102214)

Appendix: Cumberland County, Virginia, 1815 Personal Property Tax List:

Thomas Hobson District:

Persons names Chargd. with the tax [continued from prior page	Mills	Tole Bridges & ferries	Tan yards	free Male Negroes above 16	Watches guilt Silver or pinch back	Watches Single Cast Gold	Watches Double Cast Gold	livery stables & No of stalls or spaces sufficient for the accomodation of of one Horse	Houses in the Country exceeding in value $500	Tee Houses for private use	Tee Houses from which Tee is sold	Clocks clocks of wood without Case	Clocks Clocks of wood with Case
Philip Wright													
Wm Wright													
Jno W Wright													
Saymor Wright Jr													

Appendix: Cumberland County, Virginia, 1815 Personal Property Tax List:

Thomas Hobson District:

Persons names Chargd. with the tax [continued from prior page	Clocks [Cont'd]				printers & the Anuel sub-scribers to their papers	Furniture	portraits pictures prints or engrav-ings Mirror or looking Glasses piano forta harpsi-chord organ or harp
	Clocks princi-ply of Mettle	of value between 50 & 100$	of value of 100$ and upwards	Coal Pits		Business secratary or book Case Chest of drawers wardrobe or Clothe press Dining tables or separate parts there off Bedsteads side boards without drawers or dores Tea or Card tables in whole or in part Mahogany Celerel or side board with drawers or dores settee or sofa Chaires Carpits window curtains or Venetian blinds within the window of Aney House	
Philip Wright							
Wm Wright		clock taxed					
Jno W Wright							
Saymor Wright Jr							

0884(102214)

Appendix: Cumberland County, Virginia, 1815 Personal Property Tax List:

Thomas Hobson District:

Persons names Chargd. with the tax [continued from prior page	Furniture [cont'd] Bureau Secretary or Book Case Chest of drawers Warderobe or Clothes press of Aney other wood than Mahogany	Urn coffee or tea pot Candle stick Epergne or gerendole Decanter pitcher Bowl Goblets Wash Bason Stand or salver tankird Cup or Waiter	Dogs	Total amt of tax $ Cts	Identification
Philip Wright				.42	1835 Phillip W. Wright of Cumberland County, son of 1823 Saymer Wright of Cumberland County, grandson of 1770 John Wright of Cumberland County, and great grandson of 1769 George Wright of Essex County
Wm Wright				9.48	1838 William Wright of Cumberland County, son of 1774 George Wright of Cumberland County and grandson of 1769 George Wright of Essex County
Jno W Wright					1853 John Woodson Wright of Cumberland County, son of 1838 William Wright of Cumberland County, grandson of 1774 George Wright of Cumberland County, and great grandson of 1769 George Wright of Essex County
Saymor Wright Jr				.21	1815 Saymer Wright of Cumberland County, son of 1803 John Wright of Cumberland County, grandson of 1770 John Wright of Cumberland County, and great grandson of 1769 George Wright of Essex County

124.

1816 PERSONAL PROPERTY TAX LIST

CUMBERLAND COUNTY, VIRGINIA

Appendix: Cumberland County, Virginia, 1816 Personal Property Tax List:

John Baughan District:

Date of Receiving lists from Individuals	Persons Names Chargable with the tax	No of white males above 16 years old	No. Slaves above 16 years old	No of Slaves between 12 and 16 years old	No of Horses	Stud Horses No. $ Cts	4 wheeled Ri Carriages & Harness belonging thereto		Phaetons and Stage waggons and Harness belonging thereto		Coaches & Harness Belonging Thereto	
							Not exceeding in value $100 $ Cts	Exceeding in Value $100 $ Cts	Not Exceeding in Value $200 $ Cts	Exceeding in Value $200 $ Cts	Not Exceeding in Value $300 $ Cts	Exceeding in Value $300 $ Cts

[No Wrights listed]

Appendix: Cumberland County, Virginia, 1816 Personal Property Tax List:

John Baughan District:

Persons Names
Chargable with
the tax
[continued from
prior page

Total
Amount
of Taxes

Identification

[No Wrights listed]

Appendix: Cumberland County, Virginia, 1816 Personal Property Tax List:

Nathaniel Penick District:

Dates of receiving lists from individuals	Persons Names Chargable with the tax	No of white males above 16 years old	No. of Slaves above 16 years old	No of Slaves above 14 & under 16 years old	No. Horses	Stud Horses No. $ Cts	2 wheeled riding Carriages & harness belonging thereto		Phatons, Stage waggons & harness belonging thereto		Coaches & harness belonging thereto	
							Not exceeding in Value $100	Exceeding in Value $100	Not Exceeding in value $200	Exceeding in Value $200	Not Exceeding in value $300	Exceeding in Value $300
Mar 5	Seamor Wright	1	9	1	7							
Mar 5	Phillip Wright	1			2							
Mar 7	Green Wright	1	4		3				25			
Mar 25	Wm Wright	1	5	3	7							
Mar 25	Jno W. Wright	1										
Ap 12	Robt. Wright	1	3		3							
Ap 23	Geo. T. Wright	1	3	1	2							

Appendix: Cumberland County, Virginia, 1816 Personal Property Tax List:

Nathaniel Penick District:

Persons Names Chargable with the tax [continued from prior page	Total Amount of taxes	Identification
Seamor Wright	8.26	1823 Saymer Wright of Cumberland County, son of 1770 John Wright of Cumberland County and grandson of 1769 George Wright of Essex County
Phillip Wright	.36	1835 Phillip W. Wright of Cumberland County, son of 1823 Saymer Wright of Cumberland County, grandson of 1770 John Wright of Cumberland County, and great grandson of 1769 George Wright of Essex County
Green Wright	3.84	Nathaniel Green Wright of Smith County, Tennessee, son of 1831 Robert Wright of Smith County, Tennessee
Wm Wright	6.86	1838 William Wright of Cumberland County, son of 1774 George Wright of Cumberland County and grandson of 1769 George Wright of Essex County
Jno W. Wright		1853 John Woodson Wright of Cumberland County, son of 1838 William Wright of Cumberland County, grandson of 1774 George Wright of Cumberland County, and great grandson of 1769 George Wright of Essex County
Robt. Wright	2.64	1831 Robert Wright of Smith County, Tennessee
Geo. T. Wright	3.16	

130.

1817 PERSONAL PROPERTY TAX LIST

CUMBERLAND COUNTY, VIRGINIA

Appendix: Cumberland County, Virginia, 1817 Personal Property Tax List:

John Baughan District:

Date of Receiving list from Individuals	Persons Names Chargable with the Tax	No of white males above 16 years old	No. Slaves above 16 years old	No of Slaves between 12 & 16 years old	No of Horses	Stud Horses No. $ Cts	2 wheel R Carriges & Harness Belonging thereto		Phaetons & Stage waggons & harness belonging thereto		Coaches & Harness Belonging thereto	
							Not Exceeding in value $100 $ Cts	Exceeding in value $100 $ Cts	Not Exceeding in Value $200 $ Cts	Exceeding in value $200 $ Cts	Not Exceeding in value $300 $ Cts	Exceeding in value $300 $ Cts

[No Wrights listed]

Appendix: Cumberland County, Virginia, 1817 Personal Property Tax List:

John Baughan District:

Persons Names Chargable with the tax [continued from prior page	Total amount of Tax	Identification

[No Wrights listed]

Appendix: Cumberland County, Virginia, 1817 Personal Property Tax List:

Nathaniel Penick District:

Dates of receiving list from individuals	Persons names Chargable with the tax	No of White Males over 16 years old	No. of Slaves above 16 years old	No. Slaves over 12 & under 16 years old	No. Horses	Studd Horses No. $ Cts	2 Wheel riding Carriages and harness belonging thereto		Pheatons, Stage waggons & harness belonging thereto		Coaches & harness belonging thereto	
							Not exceeding in value 100	Exceeding in Value 100$	Not Exceeding in value 200	Exceeding in Value 200$	Not Exceeding in Value 300	Exceeding in Value 300$
Mar 1	Phillip Wright	1			2							
Mar 10	Seamor Wright	1	10		8							
Mar 24	Green Wright	1	4	1	3							
Mar 24	George Wright	1	2		1							
Mar 25	Robert Wright	1	2	2	4							
Mar 31	William Wright	1	6	2	6							
	John W. Wright	1			1							

0884(102214)

Appendix: Cumberland County, Virginia, 1817 Personal Property Tax List:

Nathaniel Penick District:

Persons Names Chargable with the tax [continued from prior page	Total Amount of taxes	Identification
Phillip Wright	.36	1835 Phillip W. Wright of Cumberland County, son of 1823 Saymer Wright of Cumberland County, grandson of 1770 John Wright of Cumberland County, and great grandson of 1769 George Wright of Essex County
Seamor Wright	8.44	1823 Saymer Wright of Cumberland County, son of 1770 John Wright of Cumberland County and grandson of 1769 George Wright of Essex County
Green Wright	4.04	Nathaniel Green Wright of Smith County, Tennessee, son of 1831 Robert Wright of Smith County, Tennessee
George Wright	1.58	
Robert Wright	3.52	1831 Robert Wright of Smith County, Tennessee
William Wright	6.68	1838 William Wright of Cumberland County, son of 1774 George Wright of Cumberland County and grandson of 1769 George Wright of Essex County
John W. Wright	.18	1853 John Woodson Wright of Cumberland County, son of 1838 William Wright of Cumberland County, grandson of 1774 George Wright of Cumberland County, and great grandson of 1769 George Wright of Essex County

136.

1818 PERSONAL PROPERTY TAX LIST

CUMBERLAND COUNTY, VIRGINIA

Appendix: Cumberland County, Virginia, 1818 Personal Property Tax List:

John Baughan District:

Date of Receiving list from Individuals	Persons names Chargable with the Tax	No of white males above 16 years old	No. of Slaves above 16 years old	No of Slaves between 12 & 16 years old	No. of horses	Stud Horses No. $ Cts	2 wheeled R Carriges & harness belonging thereto		Pheatons & Stage waggons & harness belonging thereto		Coaches & Harness Belonging thereto	
							Not Exceeding in value $100 $ Cts	Exceeding in value $100 $ Cts	Not Exceeding in value $200 $ Cts	Exceeding in value $200 $ Cts	Not Exceeding in value $300 $ Cts	Exceeding in value $300 $ Cts

[No Wrights listed]

Appendix: Cumberland County, Virginia, 1818 Personal Property Tax List:

<u>John Baughan District</u>:

Persons Names
Chargable with
the tax
[continued from
<u>prior page</u>

<u>Total
Amount
of Tax</u>

<u>Identification</u>

[No Wrights listed]

Appendix: Cumberland County, Virginia, 1818 Personal Property Tax List:

Nathaniel Penick District:

Dates of receiving list	Persons Names Chargable with the Tax	No. White males over 16 years	No. Slaves over 16 years old	No. Slaves over 12 & under 16	No. Horses	Studd Horses No. $ Cts	2 Wheel riding Carriages and the harness belonging thereto		Pheatons, Stage waggons and Harness belonging thereto		Coaches and harness belonging thereto	
							Not exceeding 100$ Value	Exceeding 100$ Value	Not Exceeding 200$ Value	Exceeding 200$ Value	Not Exceeding 300$ Value	Exceeding 300$ Value
Fy. 24	Green Wright	1	3		3				30			
M 10	Seamor Wright	1	10		7							
M 10	Phillip Wright	1			1							
M 30	William Wright	1	6	3	6							
M 30	John W. Wright	1			1							
A 11	Robert Wright	2	2		3							

Appendix: Cumberland County, Virginia, 1818 Personal Property Tax List:

Nathaniel Penick District:

Persons Names Chargable with the Tax [continued from prior page	Total Amount of tax $ Cents	Identification
Green Wright	3.14	Nathaniel Green Wright of Smith County, Tennessee, son of 1831 Robert Wright of Smith County, Tennessee
Seamer Wright	8.26	1823 Saymer Wright of Cumberland County, son of 1770 John Wright of Cumberland County and grandson of 1769 George Wright of Essex County
Phillip Wright	.18	1835 Phillip W. Wright of Cumberland County, son of 1823 Saymer Wright of Cumberland County, grandson of 1770 John Wright of Cumberland County, and great grandson of 1769 George Wright of Essex County
William Wright	7.38	1838 William Wright of Cumberland County, son of 1774 George Wright of Cumberland County and grandson of 1769 George Wright of Essex County
John W. Wright	.18	1853 John Woodson Wright of Cumberland County, son of 1838 William Wright of Cumberland County, grandson of 1774 George Wright of Cumberland County, and great grandson of 1769 George Wright of Essex County
Robert Wright	1.94	1831 Robert Wright of Smith County, Tennessee

142.

1819 PERSONAL PROPERTY TAX LIST

CUMBERLAND COUNTY, VIRGINIA

Appendix: Cumberland County, Virginia, 1819 Personal Property Tax List:

John Baughan District:

Date of Receiving list from Individuals	Persons names Chargable with the tax	No of white males above 16 years old	No of Slaves above 16 years old	No of Slaves between 12 & 16 years old	No. of horses	Stud horses No $ Cts	2 Wheeled R Carriges & harness belonging thereto		Phatons & Stage waggons & harness belonging thereto		Coaches &c with their harness belonging thereto	
							not ex- ceeding in value $100 $ Cts	exceed- ing in value $100 $ Cts	not ex- ceeding in value $200 $ Cts	exceed- ing in value $200 $ Cts	not ex- ceeding in value $300 $ Cts	exceed- ing in value $300 $ Cts

[No Wrights listed]

Appendix: Cumberland County, Virginia, 1819 Personal Property Tax List:

John Baughan District:

Persons Names
Chargable with
the tax
[continued from
prior page   Total amount of tax   Identification

[No Wrights listed]

Appendix: Cumberland County, Virginia, 1819 Personal Property Tax List:

<u>Nathaniel Penick District</u>:

Dates of receiving lists from individuals	Persons Names Chargable with the tax	No. white Males over 16 years	No. Slaves over 16 years	No. Slaves over 12 & under 16	No. Horses	Studd Horses No. $ Cts	2 Wheel riding Carriages and harness belonging thereto		Pheatons & Stage Waggons and harness belonging thereto		Coaches & harness belonging thereto	
							Not exceeding $100 Value	Exceeding $100 Value	Not exceeding 200$ Value	Exceeding 200$ Value	Not exceeding 300$ Value	Exceeding 300$ Value
Mar 18	Seamor Wright	1	10		4							
Mar 18	Philip Wright	1			2							
Apl 26	Wm Wright	1	6	3	6				120			
Apl 26	Jno W. Wright	1			2							

Appendix: Cumberland County, Virginia, 1819 Personal Property Tax List:

<u>Nathaniel Penick District</u>:

Persons Names Chargable with the Tax [continued from prior page	Total amount of tax $ Cents	Identification
Seamor Wright	7.72	1823 Saymer Wright of Cumberland County, son of 1770 John Wright of Cumberland County and grandson of 1769 George Wright of Essex County
Philip Wright	.36	1835 Phillip W. Wright of Cumberland County, son of 1823 Saymer Wright of Cumberland County, grandson of 1770 John Wright of Cumberland County, and great grandson of 1769 George Wright of Essex County
Wm Wright	8.08	1838 William Wright of Cumberland County, son of 1774 George Wright of Cumberland County and grandson of 1769 George Wright of Essex County
Jno W. Wright	.36	1853 John Woodson Wright of Cumberland County, son of 1838 William Wright of Cumberland County, grandson of 1774 George Wright of Cumberland County, and great grandson of 1769 George Wright of Essex County

1820 PERSONAL PROPERTY TAX LIST

CUMBERLAND COUNTY, VIRGINIA

Appendix: Cumberland County, Virginia, 1820 Personal Property Tax List:

John Baughan District:

date of Receiving list from Individuals	Persons Names Chargable with the tax	No of white males above 16 years old	No of Slaves above 16 years old	No of Slaves between 12 & 16 years old	No. of horses	Stud horses No $ Cts	2 Wheeled R Carriges & Harness belonging thereto		Phatons & S waggons & carryalls & harness Belonging thereto		Coaches Chariotts &c & harnesses belonging thereto	
							not Ex- ceeding in value $100 $ Cts	Exceed- ing in value $100 $ Cts	not ex- ceeding in value $200 $ Cts	Exceed- ing in value $200 $ Cts	not ex- ceeding in value $300 $ Cts	Exceed- ing in value $300 $ Cts

[No Wrights listed]

Appendix: Cumberland County, Virginia, 1820 Personal Property Tax List:

John Baughan District:

Persons Names
Chargable with
the tax
[continued from
prior page | Total Amount of tax | Identification

[No Wrights listed]

Appendix: Cumberland County, Virginia, 1820 Personal Property Tax List:

Nathaniel Penick District:

Dates of receiving of lists	Names of Persons Chargable with the Tax	No of white Males	No. Slaves over 16 years old	No. Slaves over 12 & under 16 yrs old	No. Horses mules &c	No. Studd Horses No. $ Cts	2 Wheel riding Carriages & harness belonging thereto		Pheatons & Stage waggons & harness belonging thereto		Coaches & harness belonging thereto	
							Not exceeding 100$ value	exceeding 100$ Value	Not exceeding 200$ Value	Exceeding 200$ Value	Not exceeding 300$ Value	Exceeding 300$ Value
Feby 28	Seamor Wright	1	10		3							
Feby 28	Phillip Wright	1			2							
Mar 17	William Wright	1	8	2	5				50			
Mar 17	John W. Wright	1			3							

Appendix: Cumberland County, Virginia, 1819 Personal Property Tax List:

Nathaniel Penick District:

Persons Names Chargable with the Tax [continued from prior page	Total amt. of taxes $ Cts	Identification
Seamor Wright	7.54	1823 Saymer Wright of Cumberland County, son of 1770 John Wright of Cumberland County and grandson of 1769 George Wright of Essex County
Phillip Wright	.36	1835 Phillip W. Wright of Cumberland County, son of 1823 Saymer Wright of Cumberland County, grandson of 1770 John Wright of Cumberland County, and great grandson of 1769 George Wright of Essex County
William Wright	8.40	1838 William Wright of Cumberland County, son of 1774 George Wright of Cumberland County and grandson of 1769 George Wright of Essex County
John W. Wright	.54	1853 John Woodson Wright of Cumberland County, son of 1838 William Wright of Cumberland County, grandson of 1774 George Wright of Cumberland County, and great grandson of 1769 George Wright of Essex County

1821 PERSONAL PROPERTY TAX LIST

CUMBERLAND COUNTY, VIRGINIA

Appendix: Cumberland County, Virginia, 1821 Personal Property Tax List:

John Baughan District:

Date of Receiving list from individuals	Persons Names Chargable with tax	Slaves above 12 years of age	Horses Mares Colts & mules	Stud horses No $ Cts	Two wheeled Riding Carriages & Harness		Phaetons & S waggons and harness		Riding Carriages and harness	
					Not Ex-ceeding in Value $100	Above the value of $100	Not ex-ceeding in Value $200	Above the value of $200	not ex-ceeding in value $300	Exceed-ing in value $300
	Saymor Wright	10	4							
	Philip Wright		3			180				
April 23	William Wright	9	5			50				
April 23	John W Wright		3							

0884(102214)

Appendix: Cumberland County, Virginia, 1821 Personal Property Tax List:

John Baughan District:

Persons Names Chargable with tax [Continued from prior page]	Amot of tax $ Cts	Identification
Saymor Wright	5.84	1823 Saymer Wright of Cumberland County, son of 1770 John Wright of Cumberland County and grandson of 1769 George Wright of Essex County
Philip Wright	1.70½	1835 Phillip W. Wright of Cumberland County, son of 1823 Saymer Wright of Cumberland County, grandson of 1770 John Wright of Cumberland County, and great grandson of 1769 George Wright of Essex County
William Wright	5.96½	1838 William Wright of Cumberland County, son of 1774 George Wright of Cumberland County and grandson of 1769 George Wright of Essex County
John W Wright	.40½	1853 John Woodson Wright of Cumberland County, son of 1838 William Wright of Cumberland County, grandson of 1774 George Wright of Cumberland County, and great grandson of 1769 George Wright of Essex County

158.

1822 PERSONAL PROPERTY TAX LIST

CUMBERLAND COUNTY, VIRGINIA

Appendix: Cumberland County, Virginia, 1822 Personal Property Tax List:

John Baughan District:

Date of Receiving list from	Persons Names Chargable with	Slaves above 12 years	Horses mares colts &	Stud horses	Two wheeled Riding Carriages & Harness		Phaetons S Waggons & tts & Harness		Riding Carriages and Harness	
					Not Ex-ceeding in value $100	Exceed-ing in value of $100	Not ex-ceeding in Value $100	Above the Value of $100	not ex-ceeding in value $200	Exceed-ing Value $200
Individuals	tax	of age	Mules	No $ Cts	$ Cts	$ Cts	$ Cts	$ Cts	$ Cts	$ Cts
April 22	Philip W Wright	1	3			170				
April 22	Saymor Wright	10	4							
April 22	John W Wright		2							
April 22	Wm Wright	10	6			50				

Appendix: Cumberland County, Virginia, 1822 Personal Property Tax List:

<u>John Baughan District</u>:

Persons Names Chargable with tax [Continued from prior page]	Amount of taxes $ Cts	Identification
Philip W Wright	2.13½	1835 Phillip W. Wright of Cumberland County, son of 1823 Saymer Wright of Cumberland County, grandson of 1770 John Wright of Cumberland County, and great grandson of 1769 George Wright of Essex County
Saymor Wright	5.84	1823 Saymer Wright of Cumberland County, son of 1770 John Wright of Cumberland County and grandson of 1769 George Wright of Essex County
John W Wright	.27	1853 John Woodson Wright of Cumberland County, son of 1838 William Wright of Cumberland County, grandson of 1774 George Wright of Cumberland County, and great grandson of 1769 George Wright of Essex County
Wm Wright	6.61	1838 William Wright of Cumberland County, son of 1774 George Wright of Cumberland County and grandson of 1769 George Wright of Essex County

162.

1823 PERSONAL PROPERTY TAX LIST

CUMBERLAND COUNTY, VIRGINIA

Appendix: Cumberland County, Virginia, 1823 Personal Property Tax List:

John Baughan District:

Date of Receiving list from Individuals	Persons Names Chargable With tax	Slaves above 12 years old	Horses Mares Colts and Mules	Stud horses No $ Cts	2 Wheeled Riding Carriages & Harness Belonging thereto and their Value $ Cts	Phaetons Stage Waggons & Carryalls & Harness and their Value $ Cts	Riding Carriages and and Harness Belonging thereto & their Value $ Cts	Amount of tax $ Cts	Identification
April 22	Philip Wright	3	4		Gigg 100			2.89	1835 Phillip W. Wright of Cumberland County, son of 1823 Saymer Wright of Cumberland County, grandson of 1770 John Wright of Cumberland County, and great grandson of 1769 George Wright of Essex County
April 28	Wm Wright	10	6		Gigg 50			5.92	1838 William Wright of Cumberland County, son of 1774 George Wright of Cumberland County and grandson of 1769 George Wright of Essex County
April 28	Jno: W Wright	1	1					.59	1853 John Woodson Wright of Cumberland County, son of 1838 William Wright of Cumberland County, grandson of 1774 George Wright of Cumberland County, and great grandson of 1769 George Wright of Essex County

0884(102214)

1824 PERSONAL PROPERTY TAX LIST

CUMBERLAND COUNTY, VIRGINIA

Appendix: Cumberland County, Virginia, 1824 Personal Property Tax List:

John Baughan District:

Date Receiving list from Individuals	Persons Names Chargable with tax	Slaves above 12 years old	Horses Mares Colts and Mules	Stud horses No $ Cts	Two wheeled Riding Carriages & Harness and their Value $ Cts	Phaetons Stage waggons & Carryalls & Harness & their value $ Cts	Other Riding Carriages & Harness and their Value $ Cts	Amount of tax $ Cts	Identification
Febry 23	Philip W Wright	6	5		Gigg 60			4.02	1835 Phillip W. Wright of Cumberland County, son of 1823 Saymer Wright of Cumberland County, grandson of 1770 John Wright of Cumberland County, and great grandson of 1769 George Wright of Essex County
April 3	George Wrights Est	11	7					6.01	
	Jno W Wright		1					.12	1853 John Woodson Wright of Cumberland County, son of 1838 William Wright of Cumberland County, grandson of 1774 George Wright of Cumberland County, and great grandson of 1769 George Wright of Essex County
	Wm Wright	10	5		Gigg 50			5.80	1838 William Wright of Cumberland County, son of 1774 George Wright of Cumberland County and grandson of 1769 George Wright of Essex County
	Pleasant Wright		1					.12	

0884(102214)

1825 PERSONAL PROPERTY TAX LIST

CUMBERLAND COUNTY, VIRGINIA

Appendix: Cumberland County, Virginia, 1825 Personal Property Tax List:

District of John Baughan:

Date Receiving list from Individuals	Persons Names Chargable with the tax	Slaves above 12 years of age	Horses Mares Colts & Mules	Stud Horses No $ Cts	Two wheeled Riding Carriages & Harness Belonging thereto and their Value $ Cts	Phaetons Stage Waggons and Carryalls and Harness Belonging thereto and their Value $ Cts	Riding Carriages and Harness Belonging thereto & their Value $ Cts	Amount of tax $ Cts	Identification
Febry 28	Philip Wright	6	5		Gigg 40			3.92	1835 Phillip W. Wright of Cumberland County, son of 1823 Saymer Wright of Cumberland County, grandson of 1770 John Wright of Cumberland County, and great grandson of 1769 George Wright of Essex County
March 1	Wm Wright Jr	1						.47	Possibly William Wright (Buckingham County), probably son of 1803 John Wright of Cumberland County, grandson of 1770 John Wright of Cumberland County, and great grandson of 1769 George Wright of Essex County
April 25	Pleasant Wright		1					.12	
April 25	Wm Wright Sr	10	6		Gig 25			5.92	1838 William Wright of Cumberland County, son of 1774 George Wright of Cumberland County and grandson of 1769 George Wright of Essex County

0884(102214)

1826 PERSONAL PROPERTY TAX LIST

CUMBERLAND COUNTY, VIRGINIA

Appendix: Cumberland County, Virginia, 1826 Personal Property Tax List:

John Baughan District:

Date Receiving list from Individuals	Persons Names Chargable with the tax	Slaves above 12 years old	Horses Mares Colts and Mules	Stud Horses No $ Cts	2 Wheeled Riding Carriages & Harness and their Value $ Cts	Phaetons Stage Waggons and Carryalls and Harness and their Value $ Cts	Riding Carriages and Harness & their Value $ Cts	Amount of tax $ Cts	Identification
Feby 4	Philip W Wright	7	5		Gigg 40			4.39	1835 Phillip W. Wright of Cumberland County, son of 1823 Saymer Wright of Cumberland County, grandson of 1770 John Wright of Cumberland County, and great grandson of 1769 George Wright of Essex County
March 27	Wm Wright	10	7		Gig 30			6.04	1838 William Wright of Cumberland County, son of 1774 George Wright of Cumberland County and grandson of 1769 George Wright of Essex County

0884(102214)

1827 PERSONAL PROPERTY TAX LIST

CUMBERLAND COUNTY, VIRGINIA

Appendix: Cumberland County, Virginia, 1827 Personal Property Tax List:

John Baughan District:

Date Receiving list from Individuals	Persons Names chargable With The Tax	Slaves above 12 years of age	Horses Mares Colts and Mules	Stud Horses No $ Cts	Two Wheeled Riding Carriages & Harness and their Value $ Cts	Phaetons Stage Waggons and Carryalls and Harness and their Value $ Cts	Riding Carriages and Harness and their Value $ Cts	Amount of tax $ Cts	Identification
March 30	Phillip W Wright	8	5		Gigg 50			4.86	1835 Phillip W. Wright of Cumberland County, son of 1823 Saymer Wright of Cumberland County, grandson of 1770 John Wright of Cumberland County, and great grandson of 1769 George Wright of Essex County
March 30	Plesant Wright		2					.24	
May 4	Wm Wright	11	7		Gig 50			6.98	1838 William Wright of Cumberland County, son of 1774 George Wright of Cumberland County and grandson of 1769 George Wright of Essex County
May 4	John W. Wright	2						.94	1853 John Woodson Wright of Cumberland County, son of 1838 William Wright of Cumberland County, grandson of 1774 George Wright of Cumberland County, and great grandson of 1769 George Wright of Essex County

0884(102214)

1828 PERSONAL PROPERTY TAX LIST

CUMBERLAND COUNTY, VIRGINIA

Appendix: Cumberland County, Virginia, 1828 Personal Property Tax List:

John Baughan District:

date Receiving list from Individuals	Persons Names Chargable With tax	Slaves above 12 years Old	Horses Mares Colts and Mules	Stud Horses	two wheeled Riding Carriages and Harness and Belonging thereto & their Value $	Phaetons, Stage Waggons and Carryalls & Harness Belonging thereto and their Value $ ¢	Other Riding Carriages and Harness Belonging thereto & their Value $ ¢	Amount Tax $ Cts	Identification
	Philip Wright	9	5		Gigg 30			5.33	1835 Phillip W. Wright of Cumberland County, son of 1823 Saymer Wright of Cumberland County, grandson of 1770 John Wright of Cumberland County, and great grandson of 1769 George Wright of Essex County
April 17	Pleasant Wright		2					.24	
April 17	John W Wright	2						.94	1853 John Woodson Wright of Cumberland County, son of 1838 William Wright of Cumberland County, grandson of 1774 George Wright of Cumberland County, and great grandson of 1769 George Wright of Essex County
May 5	Wm Wright	13	6		Gig 25			7.33	1838 William Wright of Cumberland County, son of 1774 George Wright of Cumberland County and grandson of 1769 George Wright of Essex County

0884(102214)

1829 PERSONAL PROPERTY TAX LIST

CUMBERLAND COUNTY, VIRGINIA

Appendix: Cumberland County, Virginia, 1829 Personal Property Tax List:

John Baughan District:

Date receiving list from Individuals	Persons Names Chargable with tax	Slaves above 12 years of age	Horses Mares Colts and Mules	Stud Horses N $	Two Wheeled Riding Carriages & Harness and their Value No $	Phaetons, Stage Waggons & Carryalls & Harness & their Value No $	Other Riding Carriages and Harness and their Value No $	Amount of tax $ Cts	Identification
Feby 23	Philip Wright	8	5					3.70	1835 Phillip W. Wright of Cumberland County, son of 1823 Saymer Wright of Cumberland County, grandson of 1770 John Wright of Cumberland County, and great grandson of 1769 George Wright of Essex County
April 27	Jno W Wright	2						.80	1853 John Woodson Wright of Cumberland County, son of 1838 William Wright of Cumberland County, grandson of 1774 George Wright of Cumberland County, and great grandson of 1769 George Wright of Essex County
May 4	Wm Wright	13	6		Gig 25			6.30	1838 William Wright of Cumberland County, son of 1774 George Wright of Cumberland County and grandson of 1769 George Wright of Essex County
	Pleasant Wright		2					.20	

0884(102214)

1830 PERSONAL PROPERTY TAX LIST

CUMBERLAND COUNTY, VIRGINIA

Appendix: Cumberland County, Virginia, 1830 Personal Property Tax List:

District of John Baughan:

list from Individuals	Persons Names Chargable with Tax	Slaves above 12 years of age	Horses Mares Colts & Mules	Stud Horses No $	two wheeled Riding Carriages & Harness and their Value Gigs $	Phaetons, Stage wag-gons and Carryalls and Harness & their Value Calls &c $	Riding Carriges and Harness and their Value Riding Carig $	Amount of tax $ Cts	Identification
	Philip Wright	9	5		Gig 50			4.05	1835 Phillip W. Wright of Cumberland County, son of 1823 Saymer Wright of Cumberland County, grandson of 1770 John Wright of Cumberland County, and great grandson of 1769 George Wright of Essex County
May 3	Pleasant Wright		2					.16	
May 3	John W Wright	2						.70	1853 John Woodson Wright of Cumberland County, son of 1838 William Wright of Cumberland County, grandson of 1774 George Wright of Cumberland County, and great grandson of 1769 George Wright of Essex County
May 3	Wm Wright	13	6		Gig 25			5.53	1838 William Wright of Cumberland County, son of 1774 George Wright of Cumberland County and grandson of 1769 George Wright of Essex County

0884(102214)

1831 PERSONAL PROPERTY TAX LIST

CUMBERLAND COUNTY, VIRGINIA

Appendix: Cumberland County, Virginia, 1831 Personal Property Tax List:

John Baughan District:

									Identification
April 2	John W Wright	3	2					.87	1853 John Woodson Wright of Cumberland County, son of 1838 William Wright of Cumberland County, grandson of 1774 George Wright of Cumberland County, and great grandson of 1769 George Wright of Essex County
April 30	Pleasant Wright		1					.06	
May 11	Philip Wright	8	6					2.36	1835 Phillip W. Wright of Cumberland County, son of 1823 Saymer Wright of Cumberland County, grandson of 1770 John Wright of Cumberland County, and great grandson of 1769 George Wright of Essex County
May 21	Wm Wright	11	5	Gig	20			3.55	1838 William Wright of Cumberland County, son of 1774 George Wright of Cumberland County and grandson of 1769 George Wright of Essex County

1832 PERSONAL PROPERTY TAX LIST

CUMBERLAND COUNTY, VIRGINIA

Appendix: Cumberland County, Virginia, 1832 Personal Property Tax List:

John Baughan District:

Date of Receiving list from Individuals	Persons Names Chargable with the Tax	Slaves above the age of 12	Horses Mares colts & mules	Stud Horses &c No $	two wheeled Riding Carriage & Harness belonging thereto & their Value Gigs $	Phaetons, Stage waggons & Carryalls & Harness thereto & their value Calls &c $	Riding Carriges & Harness thereto & their Value Coaches &c $	Amount of tax $ Cts	Identification
May 14	John W Wright	3	2					.87	1853 John Woodson Wright of Cumberland County, son of 1838 William Wright of Cumberland County, grandson of 1774 George Wright of Cumberland County, and great grandson of 1769 George Wright of Essex County
May 21	Wm Wright	11	5					3.05	1838 William Wright of Cumberland County, son of 1774 George Wright of Cumberland County and grandson of 1769 George Wright of Essex County
May 21	Philip Wright	10	8		Gig 50			3.48	1835 Phillip W. Wright of Cumberland County, son of 1823 Saymer Wright of Cumberland County, grandson of 1770 John Wright of Cumberland County, and great grandson of 1769 George Wright of Essex County

0884(102214)

1833 PERSONAL PROPERTY TAX LIST

CUMBERLAND COUNTY, VIRGINIA

Appendix: Cumberland County, Virginia, 1833 Personal Property Tax List:

John Baughan District:

Date of Receiving list from individuals	Persons Names Chargable with the tax	Slave above the age of 12 years	Horses Mares Colts & Mules	Stud Horses &c No $	Two Wheeled riding carriages & Harness belonging thereto & their Value No $	Phaetons, Stage Waggons & Carryalls & Harness thereto & their value No $	Four Wheeled riding carriages & Harness belonging thereto & their value No $	Amt. of tax $ ¢	Identification
_ 22	Philip Wright	9	8		Gigg 50			3.23	1835 Phillip W. Wright of Cumberland County, son of 1823 Saymer Wright of Cumberland County, grandson of 1770 John Wright of Cumberland County, and great grandson of 1769 George Wright of Essex County
Apl 1	Wm Wright	11	4					2.99	1838 William Wright of Cumberland County, son of 1774 George Wright of Cumberland County and grandson of 1769 George Wright of Essex County
Apl 1	Jno W Wright	3	2					.87	1853 John Woodson Wright of Cumberland County, son of 1838 William Wright of Cumberland County, grandson of 1774 George Wright of Cumberland County, and great grandson of 1769 George Wright of Essex County
Apl 13	Phineous G. Wright		2					.12	1844 Phineas Glover Wright of Cumberland County, son of Pryor Wright and grandson of John Wright (Bent Creek)

0884(102214)

Appendix: Cumberland County, Virginia, 1833 Personal Property Tax List:

John Baughan District:

Date of Receiving list from individuals	Persons Names Chargable with the tax	Slave above the age of 12 years	Horses Mares Colts & Mules	Stud Horses &c No $	Two Wheeled riding carriages & Harness belonging thereto & their Value No $	Phaetons, Stage Waggons & Carryalls & Harness thereto & their value No $	Four Wheeled riding carriages & Harness belonging thereto & their value No $	Amt. of tax $ ¢	Identification
May 1	Jno R Wright		1					.06	

186.

1834 PERSONAL PROPERTY TAX LIST

CUMBERLAND COUNTY, VIRGINIA

Appendix: Cumberland County, Virginia, 1834 Personal Property Tax List:

John Baughan District:

											Identification
Feby 3	John W Wright	1	2		2					.62	1853 John Woodson Wright of Cumberland County, son of 1838 William Wright of Cumberland County, grandson of 1774 George Wright of Cumberland County, and great grandson of 1769 George Wright of Essex County
Feby 3	Philip W Wright	1	8	1	7		Gig 50			3.17	1835 Phillip W. Wright of Cumberland County, son of 1823 Saymer Wright of Cumberland County, grandson of 1770 John Wright of Cumberland County, and great grandson of 1769 George Wright of Essex County
Feby 11	Pleasant Wright	2									
Feby 11	Suck Wright	1					at Creed Taylor				
Feby 11	Ryley Wright	1									
Mar 5	Wm Wright	1	12	3	5				182	4.05	1838 William Wright of Cumberland County, son of 1774 George Wright of Cumberland County and grandson of 1769 George Wright of Essex County
Apl 5	Sam Wright (F)				1						

0884(102214)

1835 PERSONAL PROPERTY TAX LIST

CUMBERLAND COUNTY, VIRGINIA

Appendix: Cumberland County, Virginia, 1835 Personal Property Tax List:

Geo C Walton District:

Date of Receiving List	Names of Persons Charged with Tax	White males over 16 years old	Slaves over 16 years old	No. Slaves between 12 & 16 years old	No Free males of Colour over 16 years	No. Horses Mares Mules & Colts	Stallons & Jacks Price of Season No $	Two wheel riding Carriages Harness Value thereof No $	Phaetons Stage waggons & Carryalls & harness & Value thereof No $	Four Wheel riding Carriages & harness Value thereof No $
	Samuel Wright					1				
	Est. Philip W Wright		8	1		7				
	John R Wright	1								
	John W Wright	1	3	1		2				
	William Wright	1	11	3		5				Car 100
	Pleasant Wright	2								

Appendix: Cumberland County, Virginia, 1835 Personal Property Tax List:

Geo C Walton District:

Names of Persons Charged with Tax [Continued from prior page]	Amot. of Tax $ ¢	Identification
Samuel Wright		
Est. Philip M Wright	2.67	Estate of 1835 Phillip W. Wright of Cumberland County, son of 1823 Saymer Wright of Cumberland County, grandson of 1770 John Wright of Cumberland County, and great grandson of 1769 George Wright of Essex County
John R Wright		
John W Wright	1.12	1853 John Woodson Wright of Cumberland County, son of 1838 William Wright of Cumberland County, grandson of 1774 George Wright of Cumberland County, and great grandson of 1769 George Wright of Essex County
William Wright	4.80	1838 William Wright of Cumberland County, son of 1774 George Wright of Cumberland County and grandson of 1769 George Wright of Essex County
Pleasant Wright		

192.

1836 PERSONAL PROPERTY TAX LIST

CUMBERLAND COUNTY, VIRGINIA

Appendix: Cumberland County, Virginia, 1836 Personal Property Tax List:

Geo C Walton District:

date of receiving taxable property from individuals	Names of persons Chargeable with Tax	No White males over 16 Years old	No Slaves over 16 Years old	No. Slaves between 12 & 16 years old	No Free Males of Colour over 16	No. Horses Mares Mules & Colts	Stallions & Jacks & price of Season No $	Two wheel riding Carriages & harness & Their Value No $	Phaetons stage waggons, Carryalls and harness & Their Value No $	Four wheel riding carriages & harness & their Value No $
	Samuel Wright					1				
	Pleasant Wright	1	1							
	Sarah Wright		9			6				
	William Wright	1	9	1		6				
	John W Wright	1	4	1		2				

Appendix: Cumberland County, Virginia, 1836 Personal Property Tax List:

Geo C Walton District:

Names of persons Chargable with Tax [Continued from prior page]	Amount of Tax paid $ ¢	Identification
Samuel Wright		
Pleasant Wright		
Sarah Wright	2.67	Sarah (_____) Wright, widow of 1835 Phillip W. Wright of Cumberland County, a son of 1823 Saymer Wright of Cumberland County, grandson of 1770 John Wright of Cumberland County, and great grandson of 1769 George Wright of Essex County
William Wright	2.86	1838 William Wright of Cumberland County, son of 1774 George Wright of Cumberland County and grandson of 1769 George Wright of Essex County
John W Wright	1.37	1853 John Woodson Wright of Cumberland County, son of 1838 William Wright of Cumberland County, grandson of 1774 George Wright of Cumberland County, and great grandson of 1769 George Wright of Essex County

196.

1837 PERSONAL PROPERTY TAX LIST

CUMBERLAND COUNTY, VIRGINIA

Appendix: Cumberland County, Virginia, 1837 Personal Property Tax List:

_____ District:

Date of receiving Lists from individuals	Names of persons Chargeable with Tax	No white Males over 16 years old	No Slaves over 16 years old	No. Slaves between 12 & 16 years old	No Free Males of Colour over 16 Years	No. Horses Mares Mules & Colts	No Stallions & Jacks and price of Season	No two wheel riding carriages and & Value thereof	No Phae-tons Stage Waggons, Carryalls & Harness & Value thereof	No four wheel pleasure carriages & harness & Value thereof
	John R Wright	1								
	Pleasant Wright	1								
	William Wright	1	10			5				Coach 400
	John W Wright	1	3			1				
	Saml Wright				1					

0884(102214)

Appendix: Cumberland County, Virginia, 1837 Personal Property Tax List:

_____ District:

Names of persons Chargable with Tax [Continued from prior page]	Amount of Tax paid	Identification
John R Wright		
Pleasant Wright		
William Wright	6.80	1838 William Wright of Cumberland County, son of 1774 George Wright of Cumberland County and grandson of 1769 George Wright of Essex County
John W Wright	.81	1853 John Woodson Wright of Cumberland County, son of 1838 William Wright of Cumberland County, grandson of 1774 George Wright of Cumberland County, and great grandson of 1769 George Wright of Essex County
Samuel Wright		

200.

1838 PERSONAL PROPERTY TAX LIST

CUMBERLAND COUNTY, VIRGINIA

Appendix: Cumberland County, Virginia, 1838 Personal Property Tax List:

_____ District:

Dates of receiving lists	Names of Persons Chargeable with Tax	No of White Males over 16 years old	No of Slaves over 16 years old	No. of Slaves between 12 & 16 years old	No Free Males of Colour over 16 Years	No. Horses Mares Mules & Colts	No Stallions and Jacks Price of Season	Two wheel riding carriages harness and Value thereof	Phaetons Stage Waggons, Carryalls & harness and Value thereof	Four wheel riding & pleasure carriages & harness and Value thereof
	Sam Wright				1					
	John R Wright	1				2				
	Pleasant Wright	1	1							
	William Wright	1	12	1		3				Coach 200
	John W Wright	1	3	2		2				

Appendix: Cumberland County, Virginia, 1838 Personal Property Tax List:

_____ District:

Names of persons Chargable with Tax [Continued from prior page]	Amount of Tax paid	Identification
Sam Wright		
John R Wright	.16	
Pleasant Wright	.30	
William Wright	6.14	1838 William Wright of Cumberland County, son of 1774 George Wright of Cumberland County and grandson of 1769 George Wright of Essex County
John W Wright	1.66	1853 John Woodson Wright of Cumberland County, son of 1838 William Wright of Cumberland County, grandson of 1774 George Wright of Cumberland County, and great grandson of 1769 George Wright of Essex County

204.

1839 PERSONAL PROPERTY TAX LIST

CUMBERLAND COUNTY, VIRGINIA

Appendix: Cumberland County, Virginia, 1839 Personal Property Tax List:

_____District:

Names of Persons Subject to pay Taxes commencing 1st March 1839	No. white Males over 16	No. Slaves over 16 years old	No. Slaves between 12 & 16	No Free males of Colour over 16	No. Horses Mares Mules & Colts	No Stallions & Jacks Price of Season	Two wheel riding Carriages & harness and value thereof	Phaetons Stage waggons & Carryalls and harness and Value thereof	Four wheel riding or pleasure Carriages & harness & Value Thereof	Amount of Goods in the possion of Merchants	Excess over $2000
Est William Wright		8			2				Coach 200		
John W Wright	1	4	1		3						
John R Wright	1	0			2						
Pleasant Wright	1	1									

Appendix: Cumberland County, Virginia, 1839 Personal Property Tax List:

_____ District:

Names of persons Subject to pay Taxes commencing 1st March 1839 [Continued from prior page]	Amount Tax paid	Identification
Est William Wright	4.56	Estate of 1838 William Wright of Cumberland County, son of 1774 George Wright of Cumberland County and grandson of 1769 George Wright of Essex County
John W Wright	1.74	1853 John Woodson Wright of Cumberland County, son of 1838 William Wright of Cumberland County, grandson of 1774 George Wright of Cumberland County, and great grandson of 1769 George Wright of Essex County
John R Wright	.16	
Pleasant Wright	.30	

1840 PERSONAL PROPERTY TAX LIST

CUMBERLAND COUNTY, VIRGINIA

Appendix: Cumberland County, Virginia, 1840 Personal Property Tax List:

_____District:

Names of Persons Chargeable with tax	No. White Males over 16	No. Slaves over 16 years old	No. Slaves between 12 & 16	No Free males of Colour over 16	No. Horses Mares Mules & Colts	No Stallions & Jacks Price of Season	Two wheel riding Carriages & harness and value thereof	Phaetons Stage waggons & Carryalls and harness and Value thereof	Four wheel riding or pleasure Carriages & harness & Value Thereof
John R Wright	1				2				
Pleasant Wright	1	2							
John W Wright	1	7	1		3				
Eliz Wright		7			2				Coach 300

0884(102214)

Appendix: Cumberland County, Virginia, 1840 Personal Property Tax List:

_____ District:

Names of persons Subject to pay Taxes commencing 1st March 1839 [Continued from prior page]	Amount Tax paid	Identification
John R Wright	.16	
Pleasant Wright	.60	
John W Wright	2.80	1853 John Woodson Wright of Cumberland County, son of 1838 William Wright of Cumberland County, grandson of 1774 George Wright of Cumberland County, and great grandson of 1769 George Wright of Essex County
Eliz Wright	.98	Elizabeth (Woodson) Wright, widow of 1838 William Wright of Cumberland County, a son of 1774 George Wright of Cumberland County and grandson of 1769 George Wright of Essex County

212.

1841 PERSONAL PROPERTY TAX LIST

CUMBERLAND COUNTY, VIRGINIA

Appendix: Cumberland County, Virginia, 1841 Personal Property Tax List:

_____ District:

Date of receiving list from individual	Persons Names Chargeable with tax	White males over sixteen	Slaves above 16 years old	Slaves above ____ years old	Free males of colour above sixteen	Horses Mares Mules & Colts	Two wheel riding carriages & value including ____	Phaetons stage ____ ____ & value including harness	Four wheel riding & carriages & value including harness
	Eliz Wright			7		2			Coach 300
	Jno W Wright	1	1	7		5			
	Pleasant Wright	1	2	2					
	John R Wright	1				1			

0884(102214)

Appendix: Cumberland County, Virginia, 1841 Personal Property Tax List:

_____ District:

Names of persons Chargable with Tax [Continued from prior page]	Amount of tax	Identification
Eliz Wright	6.80	Elizabeth (Woodson) Wright, widow of 1838 William Wright of Cumberland County, a son of 1774 George Wright of Cumberland County and grandson of 1769 George Wright of Essex County
Jno W Wright	3.82	1853 John Woodson Wright of Cumberland County, son of 1838 William Wright of Cumberland County, grandson of 1774 George Wright of Cumberland County, and great grandson of 1769 George Wright of Essex County
Pleasant Wright	1.60	
John R Wright	.12½	

216.

1842 PERSONAL PROPERTY TAX LIST

CUMBERLAND COUNTY, VIRGINIA

Appendix: Cumberland County, Virginia, 1842 Personal Property Tax List:

Hez Ford District:

Persons Names Chargeable with Tax	White Males above 16 yrs old	Slaves above 12 yrs old	Slaves above 16 yrs old	Free males of colour above 16 yrs old	Horses Mares Mules and Colts	Carriages whether 4 or 2 wheel riding Carriages, Phatons, Stage waggons Carryalls & Jersy waggons & all others with the value thereof including harness	Value of Carriages &c	Silver or Gold watches	Piano-Metallic Watches other than gold	Piano-fortes, under the value of $100	fortes, of and above the value of $100
Jno W Wright	1		7		4						
Eliz Wright			7		2	Coach	300				
Saml Wright (Sr)				1							

Appendix: Cumberland County, Virginia, 1842 Personal Property Tax List:

Hez Ford District:

Persons names chargeable with Tax [Continued from prior page]	Brass or other Metallic clocks	Gold & Silver plate, above the value of $100	Amount of Tax	Identification
Jno W Wright			3.30	1853 John Woodson Wright of Cumberland County, son of 1838 William Wright of Cumberland County, grandson of 1774 George Wright of Cumberland County, and great grandson of 1769 George Wright of Essex County
Eliz Wright	1		8.80	Elizabeth (Woodson) Wright, widow of 1838 William Wright of Cumberland County, a son of 1774 George Wright of Cumberland County and grandson of 1769 George Wright of Essex County
Saml Wright				

220.

1843 PERSONAL PROPERTY TAX LIST

CUMBERLAND COUNTY, VIRGINIA

Appendix: Cumberland County, Virginia, 1843 Personal Property Tax List:

Hez Ford District:

Persons names chargeable with tax	White Males above 16 years old	Slaves above 12 years old	Slaves above 16 years old	Free males of colour above 16 years old	Horses Mares Mules and Colts	Carriages whether 4 or 2 wheel riding carriages, phatons, stage waggons carry-alls & Jersy waggons and all others, with the value thereof, including harness	Value	Watches	Lever or Lepine Watches	Other Silver or Metallic Watches	Piano-fortes, under the value of $100	Piano-fortes, of and over the value of $100
Jno W Wright	1		9		3							
Eliz Wright			8		3	Pleasure Coach	300					1
John R Wright	1				1							
John Wright	1											

Appendix: Cumberland County, Virginia, 1843 Personal Property Tax List:

Hez Ford District:

Persons names chargeable with tax [Continued from prior page]	Metallic clocks	All other clocks	Gold & Silver plate over the value of $50	Amount of Tax	Identification
Jno W Wright		1		4.81	1853 John Woodson Wright of Cumberland County, son of 1838 William Wright of Cumberland County, grandson of 1774 George Wright of Cumberland County, and great grandson of 1769 George Wright of Essex County
Eliz Wright				10.60	Elizabeth (Woodson) Wright, widow of 1838 William Wright of Cumberland County, a son of 1774 George Wright of Cumberland County and grandson of 1769 George Wright of Essex County
John R Wright				.14	
John Wright					

1844 PERSONAL PROPERTY TAX LIST

CUMBERLAND COUNTY, VIRGINIA

Appendix: Cumberland County, Virginia, 1844 Personal Property Tax List:

Hezekiah Ford District:

Persons Chargeable with Tax	White Males above 16 yrs old	Slaves above 12 yrs old	Horses mares mules & colts	4 wheel pleasure carriages, Stages, Carryalls and 2 wheel pleasure carriages and their valuel including the harness belonging thereto	Silver patent lever or lepine watches	All other Watches	Clocks at 50 cents	Clocks at 25 cents	Pianoes under the value of $100	Pianoes of and over the value of $100	Gold and Silver plate
Jno W Wright	1	1							1		
Eliza Wright		16	6	1 4 wheel pleasure Carriage 200							
John R Wright	1		1								

Appendix: Cumberland County, Virginia, 1844 Personal Property Tax List:

Hezekiah Ford District:

Persons chargeable with tax [Continued from prior page]	Int or profits on money loaned out, profits or dividends or State or corporation bonds, and on bonds &c acquired by purchase	Physicians, surgeons Dentist & Attorneys paying Specific tax and amt of tax	Deeds, probate of Wills & letters of administration	Total amount of Tax	Identification
Jno W Wright				2.60	1853 John Woodson Wright of Cumberland County, son of 1838 William Wright of Cumberland County, grandson of 1774 George Wright of Cumberland County, and great grandson of 1769 George Wright of Essex County
Eliza Wright			2	11.15	Elizabeth (Woodson) Wright, widow of 1838 William Wright of Cumberland County, a son of 1774 George Wright of Cumberland County and grandson of 1769 George Wright of Essex County
John R Wright				.13	

INDEX

Griggs, John, 18, 74
Love, James, 18
Ransone, Geog, 83
Red, Jos., 108
Robinson, Charles, 74
Wright, Archer, 2, 9
Wright, Archibald, 12, 16, 18, 19, 24, 30, 31
Wright, Ben, 87
Wright, Benj., 79, 83
Wright, Benjamin, 42, 45, 49, 53, 56, 58, 60, 62,
  64, 66, 68, 70, 72
Wright, Benjn, 74, 75
Wright, Coleman, 82, 86
Wright, Eliz, 210, 211, 214, 215, 218, 219, 222,
  223
Wright, Eliza, 108, 226, 227
Wright, Elizabeth, 45, 56, 58, 60, 62, 64, 66
Wright, Frank, 86
Wright, Gabriel, 12, 128
Wright, George, 2, 4, 5, 6, 8, 13, 18, 25, 30, 31,
  134, 135, 166
Wright, Green, 91, 95, 128, 134, 135, 140, 141
Wright, Griffin, 2
Wright, Henry, 2
Wright, Jacob, 16, 18, 19, 22, 23, 28, 29, 40, 41,
  44
Wright, James, 18
Wright, Jno R, 185
Wright, Jno W, 112, 113, 120, 121, 122, 123,
  128, 146, 147, 164, 166, 176, 184, 214, 215,
  218, 219, 222, 223, 226, 227
Wright, John, 2, 4, 5, 6, 8, 12, 16, 18, 19, 24, 30,
  31, 36, 37, 42, 45, 49, 53, 56, 58, 60, 62, 64,
  66, 68, 70, 74, 222, 223

Wright, John R, 190, 191, 198, 199, 201, 203,
  206, 207, 210, 211, 214, 215, 222, 223, 226,
  227
Wright, John W, 156, 157, 160, 161, 174, 178,
  180, 182, 188, 190, 191, 194, 195, 198, 199,
  201, 203, 206, 207, 210, 211, 134, 135, 140,
  141, 152, 153, 172
Wright, Mary, 36, 37
Wright, Nancy, 72, 74, 75
Wright, Paul, 22, 23, 28, 29, 40, 41, 44
Wright, Philip, 120, 121, 122, 123, 146, 147, 156,
  157, 164, 168, 174, 176, 178, 180, 182, 184
Wright, Philip M, 191
Wright, Philip W, 160, 161, 166, 170, 188, 190
Wright, Phillip, 128, 134, 135, 140, 141, 152, 153
Wright, Phillip W, 172
Wright, Phineous G., 184
Wright, Pleasant, 166, 168, 174, 176, 178, 180,
  188, 190, 191, 194, 195, 198, 199, 201, 203,
  206, 207, 210, 211, 214, 215
Wright, Plesant, 172
Wright, Robert, 134, 135, 140, 141
Wright, Robt., 128
Wright, Ryley, 188
Wright, Sam, 188, 201, 203
Wright, Saml, 79, 83, 108, 198
Wright Sr, Saml, 218, 219
Wright, Samuel, 60, 62, 64, 66, 68, 70, 72, 190,
  191, 194, 195, 199
Wright, Sarah, 194, 195
Wright, Saymer, 74, 75, 95, 99, 103, 108, 156,
  157, 160, 161
Wright jr, Saymer, 74
Wright, Saymore, 12, 16, 18, 19, 24, 30, 31, 36,
  37, 42, 45, 49, 53, 56, 58, 60, 62, 64, 66, 68,
  70, 72, 87
Wright Jr, Saymor, 120, 121, 122, 123

Wright, Saymour, 112, 113, 141, 128, 134, 135,
  140, 146, 147, 152, 153
Wright, Seaymour, 79, 83
Wright, Seymer, 8
Wright, Seymore, 2, 4, 5, 6
Wright, Suck, 188
Wright, Thomas, 2, 4, 5, 6, 8, 12, 16, 18, 19, 24,
  30, 31, 36, 37, 42, 49, 53
Wright, William, 2, 4, 5, 6, 8, 12, 30, 31, 36, 37,
  42, 45, 49, 53, 56, 58, 60, 62, 64, 66, 68, 70,
  72, 91, 95, 134, 135, 140, 141, 152153, 156,
  157, 190, 191, 194, 195, 198, 199, 201, 203,
  206, 207
Wright, Wm, 74, 75, 79, 87, 103, 108, 112, 113,
  120, 121, 122, 123, 128, 146, 147, 160, 161,
  164, 166, 170, 172, 174, 176, 178, 180, 182,
  184, 188
Wright Jr, Wm, 168

0884(102214)

228.

WRIGHT FAMILY

CENSUS RECORDS

1810 Through 1900

CUMBERLAND COUNTY, VIRGINIA

Revised as of October 23, 2014

© 2014, Robert N. Grant
0391(102314)

Introduction To Appendix: 1810 Through 1900 Censuses, Cumberland County, Virginia

This document is an appendix to a larger work titled Sorting Some Of The Wrights Of Southern Virginia. The work is divided into parts for each family of Wrights that has been researched. Each part is divided into two sections; the first section is text discussing the family and the evidence supporting the relationships and the second section is a descendants chart summarizing the relationships and information known about each individual.

The appendices to the work (of which this document is one) present source records for persons named Wright by county and by type of record with the identification of the person named and their Wright ancestors to the extent known.

The sources for the records listed in this appendix are the following:

1) 1810 to 1900 Censuses, Cumberland County, Virginia, microfilm copies available at National Archives - Pacific Sierra Division, 1000 Commodore Drive, San Bruno, California 94066 and at Ancestry.com.

The identification of a person or their ancestor by year and county indicates their year of death and county of residence at death. For example, "1763 Thomas Wright of Bedford County" indicates that this was the Thomas Wright who died in 1763 in Bedford County. If no state is listed after the county, the state is Virginia; counties in states other than Virginia will have a state listed after the county, as in "1876 William S. Wright of Highland County, Ohio".

A parenthetical after the name indicates an identification of the person when a place of death is not yet known, as in "John Wright (Goochland County Carpenter)". A county in parentheses after the name indicates the county with which that person was most identified when no evidence of the place of death has yet been found, as in "Grief Wright (Bedford County)".

All or portions of the text and descendants charts for each Wright family identified are available from the author:

Robert N. Grant
15 Campo Bello Court
Menlo Park, California 94025
(H) 650-854-0895
(O) 650-614-3800

This is a work in process and I would be most interested in receiving additional information about any of the persons identified in these records in order to correct any errors or expand on the information given.

0391(102314)

APPENDIX:

1810 CENSUS

CUMBERLAND COUNTY, VIRGINIA

Appendix: Cumberland County, Virginia, 1810 Census:

Name of Town, city or County	Names of Heads of families	Free White Males					Free White Females				
		Under ten years of age to 10	Of ten years, and under sixteen to 16	Of sixteen and under twenty-six including heads of families to 26	Of twenty-six and under forty-five including heads of families to 45	Of forty five and upwards, including heads of families 45&c	Under ten years of age to 10	Of ten years, and under sixteen to 16	Of sixteen, and under twenty six including heads of families to 26	Of twenty-six and under forty five, including heads of families to 45	Of forty-five and upwards, including heads of families 45&c
	Green Right				1		1		1		
	Seaymore Right jr			2	1						
	Seaymore Right			2		1					
	William Right		1			1				1	

0391(122113)

Appendix: Cumberland County, Virginia, 1810 Census:

Names of Heads of families [continued from prior page]	All other free persons except Indians, not taxed	Slaves	Identification
Green Wright		7	Nathaniel Green Wright of Smith County, Tennessee, son of 1831 Robert Wright of Smith County, Tennessee
Seaymore Right jr		5	1815 Saymer Wright of Cumberland County, son of 1803 John Wright of Cumberland County, grandson of 1770 John Wright of Cumberland County, and great grandson of 1769 George Wright of Essex County
Seaymore Right		12	1823 Saymer Wright of Cumberland County, son of 1770 John Wright of Cumberland County and grandson of 1769 George Wright of Essex County
William Right		12	

0391(122113)

APPENDIX:

1820 CENSUS

CUMBERLAND COUNTY, VIRGINIA

Appendix: Cumberland County, Virginia, 1820 Census:

Names of Heads of Families	Free White Males						Free White Females				
	Free white males under ten years to 10	Free white males under and under sixteen to 16	Free white males between sixteen and eighteen 16 to 18	Free white males of sixteen and and under twenty-six including heads of families 16 to 26	Free white males of twenty-six and under forty-five, including heads of families to 45	Free white males of forty-five and upwards, including heads of families 45, &c.	Free white females under ten years of age to 10	Free white females of ten and under sixteen to 16	Free white females of sixteen and under twenty six, including heads of families to 26	Free white females of twenty-six and under forty-five, including heads of families to 45	Free white females of forty-five, and upwards including heads of families 45, &c.
William Wright	0	0	0	0	1	1	1	0	0	1	1
Seymore Wright	0	0	0	0	1	1	0	0	0	0	

Appendix: Cumberland County, Virginia, 1820 Census:

Names of Heads of Families [continued from prior page]	Foreigners not natur- alized	Number of persons engaged in Agri- culture	Number of persons engaged in Commerce	Number of persons engaged in Manu- facture	Slaves							
					Males				Females			
					Males under fourteen to 14	Males of fourteen and under twenty-six to 26	Males of twenty-six and under forty-five to 45	Males of forty-five and upwards 45, &c.	Females of (under) fourteen to 14	Females of fourteen and under twenty-six to 26	Females of twenty-six and under forty-five to 45	Females of forty- five and upwards 45, &c.
William Wright	0	8	0	0	4	0	1	0	2	0	0	0
Seymore Wright	[unreadable]											

0391(122113)

Appendix: Cumberland County, Virginia, 1820 Census:

Names of Heads of Families [continued from prior page]	Free Colored Persons								All others except Indians not taxed	Identification
	Males				Females					
	Males under fourteen years to 14	Males of fourteen and under twenty-six to 26	Males of twenty-six and under forty-five to 45	Males of forty five and upwards 45, &c	Females under fourteen years to 14	Females of fourteen and under twenty-six to 26	Females of twenty-six and under forty-five to 45	Females of forty-five and upwards 45, &c		
William Wright										1838 William Wright of Cumberland County, son of 1774 George Wright of Cumberland County and grandson of 1769 George Wright of Essex County
Seymore Wright										1823 Saymer Wright of Cumberland County, son of 1770 John Wright of Cumberland County and grandson of 1769 George Wright of Essex County

APPENDIX:

1830 CENSUS

CUMBERLAND COUNTY, VIRGINIA

Appendix: Cumberland County, Virginia, 1830 Census

Names Heads of Families	Free White Persons (including heads of families) Males												
	Under five years of age under 5	Of five and under ten 5 to 10	Of ten and under fifteen 10 to 15	Of fifteen and under twenty 15 to 20	Of twenty and under thirty 20 to 30	Of thirty and under forty 30 to 40	Of forty and under fifty 40 to 50	Of fifty and under sixty 50 to 60	Of sixty and under seventy 60 to 70	Of seventy and under eighty 70 to 80	Of eighty and under ninety 80 to 90	Of ninety and under one hundred 90 to 100	Of one hundred and upwards 100, &c.
Philip W Wright	0	0	0	0	1	1	0	0	0	0	0	0	0
William R Wright	0	0	0	0	1	0	0	0	0	0	0	0	0
John W Wright	1	0	0	0	0	1	0	0	0	0	0	0	0
William Wright	0	0	0	0	0	0	0	0	0	1	0	0	0
Pleasant Wright	0	0	1	1	1	0	0	1	0	0	0	0	0
Samuel Wright	0	0	0	0	0	0	0	0	0	0	0	0	0

Appendix: Cumberland County, Virginia, 1830 Census

Names Heads of Families [Continued from prior page]	Free White Persons (including heads of families) [Continued] Females												
	Under five years of age under 5	Of five and under ten 5 to 10	Of ten and under fifteen 10 to 15	Of fifteen and under twenty 15 to 20	Of twenty and under thirty 20 to 30	Of thirty and under forty 30 to 40	Of forty and under fifty 40 to 50	Of fifty and under sixty 50 to 60	Of sixty and under seventy 60 to 70	Of seventy and under eighty 70 to 80	Of eighty and under ninety 80 to 90	Of ninety and under one hundred 90 to 100	Of one hundred and upwards 100, &c.
Philip W Wright	0	0	0	1	1	1	0	0	0	0	0	0	0
William R Wright	0	0	0	1	0	0	0	0	0	0	0	0	0
John W Wright	0	2	0	0	1	0	0	0	0	0	0	0	0
William Wright	0	0	0	0	0	0	0	1	0	0	0	0	0
Pleasant Wright	1	0	0	0	1	0	1	0	0	0	0	0	0
Samuel Wright	0	0	0	0	0	0	0	0	0	0	0	0	0

Appendix: Cumberland County, Virginia, 1830 Census

Names Heads of Families [Continued from prior page]	Slaves											
	Males						Females					
	Under ten years of age under 10	Of ten and under twenty-four 10 to 24	Of twenty-four and under thirty-six 24 to 36	Of thirty-six and under fifty-five 36 to 55	Of fifty-five and under one hundred 55 to 100	Of one hundred and upwards 100, &c	Under ten years of age under 10	Of ten and under twenty-four 10 to 24	Of twenty-four and under thirty-six 24 to 36	Of thirty-six and under fifty-five 36 to 55	Of fifty-five and under one hundred 55 to 100	Of one hundred and upwards 100, &c
Philip W Wright	0	3	4	1	0	0	0	2	0	1	0	0
William R Wright	0	0	0	0	0	0	0	0	0	0	0	0
John W Wright	3	0	0	0	0	0	1	1	1	0	0	0
William Wright	10	5	2	1	1	0	3	4	3	2	0	0
Pleasant Wright	0	0	0	0	0	0	0	1	0	0	0	0
Samuel Wright	0	0	0	0	0	0	0	0	0	0	0	0

Appendix: Cumberland County, Virginia, 1830 Census

	Free Colored Persons											
	Males						Females					
Names Heads of Families [Continued from prior page]	Under ten years of age under 10	Of ten and under twenty-four 10 to 24	Of twenty-four and under thirty-six 24 to 36	Of thirty-six and under fifty-five 36 to 55	Of fifty-five and under one hundred 55 to 100	Of one hundred and upwards 100, &c	Under ten years of age under 10	Of ten and under twenty-four 10 to 24	Of twenty-four and under thirty-six 24 to 36	Of thirty-six and under fifty-five 36 to 55	Of fifty-five and under one hundred 55 to 100	Of one hundred and upwards 100, &c
Philip W Wright	0	0	0	0	0	0	0	0	0	0	0	0
William R Wright	0	0	0	0	0	0	0	0	0	0	0	0
John W Wright	0	0	0	0	0	0	0	0	0	0	0	0
William Wright	0	0	0	0	0	0	0	0	0	0	0	0
Pleasant Wright	0	0	0	0	0	0	0	0	0	0	0	0
Samuel Wright	0	0	0	1	0	0	0	0	0	0	0	0

Appendix: Cumberland County, Virginia, 1830 Census

Names Heads of Families [Continued from prior page]	Total	White Persons included in the foregoing					Slaves and Colored Persons, included in the foregoing		
		Who are Deaf and Dumb, under fourteen years of age under 14	Who are Deaf and Dumb, of the age of fourteen and under twenty-five 14 to 25	Who are Deaf and Dumb, of twenty-five and upwards 25, &c.	Who are blind	Aliens - Foreigners and naturalized	Who are Deaf and Dumb, under fourteen years of age under 14	Who are Deaf and Dumb, of the age of fourteen and under twenty-five 14-25	Who are Deaf and Dumb of twenty-five and upwards 25, &c.	Who are blind
Philip W Wright	16									
William R Wright	2									
John W Wright	11									
William Wright	32									
Pleasant Wright	8									
Samuel Wright	1									

Appendix: Cumberland County, Virginia, 1830 Census

| Names
Heads of Families
[Continued from
prior page]	Identification
Philip W Wright	1835 Phillip W. Wright of Cumberland County, son of 1823 Saymer Wright of Cumberland County, grandson of 1770 John Wright of Cumberland County, and great grandson of 1769 George Wright of Essex County
William R Wright	
John W Wright	1853 John Woodson Wright of Cumberland County, son of 1838 William Wright of Cumberland County, grandson of 1774 George Wright of Cumberland County, and great grandson of 1769 George Wright of Essex County
William Wright	1838 William Wright of Cumberland County, son of 1774 George Wright of Cumberland County and grandson of 1769 George Wright of Essex County
Pleasant Wright	
Samuel Wright	

0391(122113)

APPENDIX:

1840 CENSUS

CUMBERLAND COUNTY, VIRGINIA

Appendix: Cumberland County, Virginia, 1840 Census

| Names of Heads of Families | Free White Persons (including heads of families) Males | | | | | | | | | | | | |
	Under 5	5 & under 10	10 & under 15	15 & under 20	20 & under 30	30 & under 40	40 & under 50	50 & under 60	60 & under 70	70 & under 80	80 & under 90	90 & under 100	100 and upwards
Pleasant Wright	0	0	1	0	1	0	0	0	1	0	0	0	0
John W Wright	0	1	2	0	0	0	1	0	0	0	0	0	0
Elizabeth Wright	0	0	0	0	0	0	0	0	0	0	0	0	0

0391(122113)

Appendix: Cumberland County, Virginia, 1840 Census

| Names of Heads of Families [Continued from prior page] | Free White Persons (including heads of families) [Continued] ||||||||||||
| | Females ||||||||||||
	Under 5	5 & under 10	10 & under 15	15 & under 20	20 & under 30	30 & under 40	40 & under 50	50 & under 60	60 & under 70	70 & under 80	80 & under 90	90 & under 100	100 and upwards
Pleasant Wright	0	2	0	2	0	0	0	1	0	0	0	0	0
John W Wright	1	1	0	2	0	1	0	0	0	0	0	0	0
Elizabeth Wright	0	0	0	0	0	0	0	0	1	0	0	0	0

Appendix: Cumberland County, Virginia, 1840 Census

| | | Free Colored Persons | | | | | | | | | | |
| | | Males | | | | | | Females | | | | |
Names of Heads of Families [Continued from prior page]	Under 10	10 & under 24	24 & under 36	36 & under 55	55 & under 100	100 & and upwards	5 & under 10	10 & under 24	24 & under 36	36 & under 55	55 & under 100	100 and upwards
Pleasant Wright												
John W Wright												
Elizabeth Wright												

Appendix: Cumberland County, Virginia, 1840 Census

Names of Heads of Families [Continued from prior page]	Slaves												
	Males						Females						
	Under 10	10 & under 24	24 & under 36	36 & under 55	55 & under 100	100 and upwards	Under 10	10 & under 24	24 & under 36	36 & under 55	55 & under 100	100 and upwards	Total
Pleasant Wright	3	0	0	0	0	0	3	0	2	0	0	0	16
John W Wright	1	2	1	2	0	0	2	2	3	1	1	0	24
Elizabeth Wright	1	2	3	1	0	0	3	1	3	1	0	0	15

0391(122113)

Appendix: Cumberland County, Virginia, 1840 Census

| Names of Heads of Families [Continued from prior page] | Number of Persons in each Family Employed in | | | | | | | Pensioners for Revolutionary or Military Services Included in the foregoing | | Deaf and Dumb, Blind and Insane White Persons Included in the Foregoing | | | | | |
| | | | | | | | | | | Deaf and Dumb | | | | Insane and Idiots | |
	Mining	Agri-culture	Commerce	Manu-facture and trades	Navi-gation of the ocean	Navi-gation of canals lakes and rivers	Learned profes-sions and en-gineers	Names	Ages	Under 14	14 & under 25	25 and upwards	Blind	Insane and idiots at public charge	Insane and idiots at private charge
Pleasant Wright				2											
John W Wright		3					1								
Elizabeth Wright		5													

Appendix: Cumberland County, Virginia, 1840 Census

Names of Heads of Families [Continued from prior page]	Deaf and Dumb, Blind and Insane Colored Persons Included in the Foregoing				Schools, &c.						
	Deaf, Dumb, and Blind		Insane and Idiots								
	Deaf & Dumb	Blind	Insane and idiots at private charge	Insane and idiots at public charge	Universities or College	Number of Students	Academies & Grammar Schools	No. of Scholars	Primary and Common Schools	No. of Scholars	No. of Scholars at public charge
Pleasant Wright											
John W Wright											
Elizabeth Wright											

Appendix: Cumberland County, Virginia, 1840 Census

Names of Heads of Families [Continued from prior page]	No. of white persons over 90 years of age in each family who cannot read or write	Identification
Pleasant Wright		
John W Wright		1853 John Woodson Wright of Cumberland County, son of 1838 William Wright of Cumberland County, grandson of 1774 George Wright of Cumberland County, and great grandson of 1769 George Wright of Essex County
Elizabeth Wright		Elizabeth (Woodson) Wright, widow of 1838 William Wright of Cumberland County, a son of 1774 George Wright of Cumberland County and grandson of 1769 George Wright of Essex County

0391(122113)

APPENDIX:

1850 CENSUS

CUMBERLAND COUNTY, VIRGINIA

Appendix: Cumberland County, Virginia, 1850 Census

Name	Age	Sex	Color	Occupation	Value of Real Estate	Place of Birth	Married Within Year	Attended School Within Year	Cannot Read & Write	Deaf Dumb Blind Insane etc.	Identification
08/07/1850 134/134											
Thomas Wright	35	M		Overseer		Virginia					
Ann Wright	23	F				Virginia					
Charles Wright	4	M				Virginia					
09/24/1850 466/466											
John W. Wright	56	M		Farmer	215	Virginia					1853 John Woodson Wright of Cumberland
Nancy Wright	49	F				Virginia					County, son of 1838 William Wright of
Sarah E Wright	28	F				Virginia					Cumberland County, grandson of 1774 George
Margaret D Wright	26	F				Virginia					Wright of Cumberland County and great
James Wright	21	M		Clerk		Virginia					grandson of 1769 George Wright of Essex
Ivanna F. Wright	18	F				Virginia					County
Nathaniel Wright	16	M		Student		Virginia		1			
Ann A Wright	13	F				Virginia		1			
Nina L Wright	6	F				Virginia					
10/04/1850 581/581											
William B Anderson	41	M		Farmer	500	Virginia					
William B Anderson	17	M		Farmer		Virginia					
Mary E Wright	15	F				Virginia					
Susan Anderson	8	F				Virginia					

0391(122113)

APPENDIX:

1860 CENSUS

CUMBERLAND COUNTY, VIRGINIA

Appendix: Cumberland County, Virginia, 1860 Census

Name	Age	Sex	Color	Occupation	Value of Real Estate	Value of Personal Property	Place of Birth	Married Within Year	Attended School Within Year	Cannot Read & Write	Deaf Dumb Blind Insane etc.	Identification
377/380 07/13/1860												
Billy Smith	35	M	M	Laborer			Virginia					1898 Seymore A. Wright of
Semere Wright	40	M		Miller		60	Virginia					Amelia County, son of 1863
Catharine Wright	30	F					Virginia					William Wright of Buckingham
Sarah Wright	15	F					Virginia					County, probably grandson of
William S. Wright	13	M					Virginia		1			1803 John Wright of Cumberland
Thomas H Wright	12	M					Virginia		1			County, great grandson of 1770
John S Wright	10	M					Virginia		1			John Wright of Cumberland
James A. Wright	8	M					Virginia					County and great great grandson
Edward F Wright	5	M					Virginia					of 1769 George Wright of Essex
Philip Wright	1	M					Virginia					County

APPENDIX:

1870 CENSUS

CUMBERLAND COUNTY, VIRGINIA

Appendix: Cumberland County, Virginia, 1870 Census

Name	Age	Sex	Color	Occupation	Value of Real Estate	Value of Personal Property	Place of Birth	Married Within Year	Born Within Year	Attended School Within Year	Cannot Read	Cannot Write	Deaf Dumb Blind Insane or or Idiot
140/172 07/08/1870													
John R. Palmore	28	M	W	ret. dealer	1500	700	Virginia						
N. A. Dowdy	26	M	W	Clerk in Mill		120	Virginia						
Simon Wright	52	M	W	Miller		500	Virginia						
John G. Ayres	50	M	W	Cooper			Virginia						
281/324 07/20/1870													
Robert Goodman	62	M	W	Farmer			Virginia						
Frances Goodman	52	F	W	Keeping house	700		Virginia						
Burley Goodman	24	M	W	Physician		350	Virginia						
Henry Goodman	32	M	W	Teacher			Virginia						
Lilia Goodman	16	F	W	Teacher			Virginia						
Molly Goodman	14	F	W	At home			Virginia						
Ann Wright	43	F	W	At home			Virginia						
George Wright	10	M	W				Virginia						
Louise Meador	15	F	B	Domestic Servant			Virginia				1	1	
Julia Meador	40	F	B	Cook			Virginia				1	1	
Michael Meador	12	M	B	Doemstic Servant			Virginia				1	1	
146/154 08/09/1870													
Simon Wright	50	M	B	Farm Laborer			Virginia				1	1	
Nancy Wright	25	F	B	Keeping house			Virginia				1	1	
John Wright	2	M	B				Virginia						
199/210 08/11/1870													
Hal Wright	50	M	B	Farm Laborer			Virginia				1	1	
Sophie Wright	33	F	B	Keeping house			Virginia				1	1	
Edmund Wright	21	M	B	Farm Laborer			Virginia				1	1	

Appendix: Cumberland County, Virginia, 1870 Census

Name [Continued from prior page]	Male Citizen Over 21	Male Citizen Over 21 Without Right to Vote	Identification
140/172 07/08/1870			
John R. Palmore	1		1898 Seymore A. Wright of Amelia County, son of 1863 William Wright of Buckingham County, probably grandson of 1803 John Wright of Cumberland County, great grandson of 1770 John Wright of Cumberland County, and great great grandson of 1769 George Wright of Essex County
N. A. Dowdy	1		
Simon Wright	1		
John G. Ayres	1		
281/324 07/20/1870			
Robert Goodman	1		
Frances Goodman			
Burley Goodman	1		
Henry Goodman	1		
Lilia Goodman			
Molly Goodman			
Ann Wright			
George Wright			
Louise Meador			
Julia Meador			
Michael Meador			
146/154 08/09/1870			
Simon Wright			
Nancy Wright			
John Wright	1		
199/210 08/11/1870			
Hal Wright	1		
Sophie Wright			
Edmund Wright	1		

Appendix: Cumberland County, Virginia, 1870 Census

Name	Age	Sex	Color	Occupation	Value of Real Estate	Value of Personal Property	Place of Birth	Married Within Year	Born Within Year	Attended School Within Year	Cannot Read	Cannot Write	Deaf Dumb Blind Insane or or Idiot
203/214 08/11/1870													
Wyatt Wright	33	M	B	Farm laborer			Virginia				1	1	
Agnes Wright	30	F	B	Keeping house			Virginia				1	1	
Sophie Wright	7	F	B				Virginia						
Mary Wright	4	F	B				Virginia						
Louisa Wright	2	F	B				Virginia						

0391(122113)

Appendix: Cumberland County, Virginia, 1870 Census

Name [Continued from prior page]	Male Citizen Over 21	Male Citizen Over 21 Without Right to Vote	Identification
203/214 08/11/1870			
Wyatt Wright	1		
Agnes Wright			
Sophie Wright			
Mary Wright			
Louisa Wright			

APPENDIX:

1880 CENSUS

CUMBERLAND COUNTY, VIRGINIA

Appendix: Cumberland County, Virginia, 1880 Census

Name	Color	Sex	Age	Month of Birth	Relationship	Marital Status	Married During Year	Occupation	Months Unemployed	Sickness Blind Deaf & Dumb Idiotic Disabled

Hamilton District
24th day of June, 1880

Dwelling #319/Family #394

Name	Color	Sex	Age	Month of Birth	Relationship	Marital Status	Married During Year	Occupation	Months Unemployed	Sickness Blind Deaf & Dumb Idiotic Disabled
Maria Bundrant	B	F	46			W/D		Laborer		
William Wright	Mu	M	14		grandson	S		Laborer		
Cornelius Sales	B	M	40		Boarder	S		Laborer		

Madison District
2 day of June 1880

Dwelling #41/Family #43

Name	Color	Sex	Age	Month of Birth	Relationship	Marital Status	Married During Year	Occupation	Months Unemployed	Sickness Blind Deaf & Dumb Idiotic Disabled
Robt J Goodman	W	M	72			M		Farmer		
Frances W Goodman	W	F	62		Wife	M		Keeping house		
Ann Wright	W	F	44		boarder	W/D		No occupation		
Geoge Wright	W	M	21		Son	S		works on farm		
William Wright	W	M	18		Son	S		works on farm		

Randolph District
28th day of June, 1880

Dwelling #521/Family #521

Name	Color	Sex	Age	Month of Birth	Relationship	Marital Status	Married During Year	Occupation	Months Unemployed	Sickness Blind Deaf & Dumb Idiotic Disabled
Simon Wright	B	M	50			M		Farmer		
Pattie Wright	B	F	40		wife	M		Keeping house		
Davie Gray	B	M	30		Boarder	M		Farm hand		
Martha Gray	B	F	40		Boarder	M		Keeping house		
Sam Gray	B	M	2		Boarder	S				

Appendix: Cumberland County, Virginia, 1880 Census

Name [continued from previous page]	Attended School Within Year	Cannot Read	Cannot Write	Born	Father Born	Mother Born	Identification
Hamilton District **24th day of June, 1880**							
Dwelling #319/Family #394							
Maria Bundrant		1	1	Virginia	Va	Va	
William Wright	1			Virginia	Virginia	Virginia	
Cornelius Sales		1	1	Virginia	Va	Va	
Madison District **2 day of June 1880**							
Dwelling #41/Family #43							
Robt J Goodman				Virginia	Va	Va	
Frances W Goodman				Virginia	Va	Va	
Ann Wright				Virginia	Va	Va	
Geoge Wright				Virginia	Va	Va	
William Wright				Virginia	Va	Va	
Randolph District **28th day of June, 1880**							
Dwelling #521/Family #521							
Simon Wright		1	1	Va	Va	Va	
Pattie Wright		1	1	Va	Va	Va	
Davie Gray		1	1	Va	Va	Va	
Martha Gray		1	1	Va	Va	Va	
Sam Gray				Va	Va	Va	

0391(122113)

Appendix: Cumberland County, Virginia, 1880 Census

Name	Color	Sex	Age	Month of Birth	Relationship	Marital Status	Married During Year	Occupation	Months Unemployed	Sickness Blind Deaf & Dumb Idiotic Disabled
Dwelling #544/Family #544										
Edmond Wright	B	M	30			M		Farm hand		
Cary Wright	B	F	32		wife	M		Keeping house		
Martha Wright	B	F	6		Niece					

Appendix: Cumberland County, Virginia, 1880 Census

Name [continued from previous page]	Attended School Within Year	Cannot Read	Cannot Write	Born	Father Born	Mother Born	Identification
Dwelling #544/Family #544							
Edmond Wright			1	Va	Va	Va	
Cary Wright			1	Va	Va	Va	
Martha Wright				Virginia	Virginia	Virginia	

0391(122113)

1900 CENSUS

CUMBERLAND COUNTY, VIRGINIA

Appendix: Cumberland County, Virginia, 1900 Census

In Cities Street	House Number	Number of dwelling houses in the order of visitation	Number of family in the order of visitation	Name of each person whose place of abode on June 1, 1900, was in this family.	Relationship of each person to the head the family	Color or race	Sex	Date of Birth Month	Year	Age at last birthday	Whether single, married, widowed, or divorced	Number of years married	Mother of how many children	Number of these children living
June 7, 1900														
		49	49	George Wright	Head	W	M		1850	50	M	20	.	.
				Pattie Wright	Wife	W	F		1857	43	M	20	7	7
				William Wright	Son	W	M		1882	18	S	.	.	.
				Emeline Wright	Daughter	W	F		1883	17	S	.	.	.
				Oscar Wright	Son	W	M		1886	14	S	.	.	.
				Mattie Wright	Daughter	W	F		1888	12	S	.	.	.
				Allomillia Wright	Daughter	W	F		1891	9	S	.	.	.
				Ben Wright	Son	W	M		1893	7	S	.	.	.
				Hattie Wright	Daughter	W	F		1894	5	S	.	.	.
June 9, 1900														
		78	78	Randal Bryant	Head	B	M	May	1825	75	M	20	.	.
				Julia A Bryant	Wife	B	F	June	1826	73	M	20	18	6
				India Wright	Granddaughter	B	F	Jan	1870	30	S	.	.	.
				Mattie Brown	Granddaughter	B	F	June	1884	15	S	.	.	.
				Maud Agee	Granddaughter	B	F	Apr	1890	10	S	.	.	.
				London Wright	Grandson	B	M	June	1892	7	S	.	.	.
				Ernest Wright	Grandson	B	M	July	1894	5	S	.	.	.
				Eddie Wilkinson	Boarder	B	M	May	1873	27	S	.	.	.

Appendix: Cumberland County, Virginia, 1900 Census

Name of each person whose place of abode on June 1, 1900, was in this family. [continued from prior page]	Nativity			Citizenship			Occupation, Trade, Or Profession of each person Ten Years of age and over.		Education			
	Place of birth of each person and parents of each person enumerated											
	Place of birth of this Person	Place of birth of Father of this person	Place of birth of Mother of this person	Year of immigration to the United States	Number of years in the United States	Natural-ization	Occupation	Months not employed	Attended school in months)	Can read	Can write	Can speak English

June 7, 1900

George Wright	Virginia	Virginia	Virginia									
Pattie Wright	Virginia	Virginia	Virginia									
William Wright	Virginia	Virginia	Virginia									
Emeline Wright	Virginia	Virginia	Virginia									
Oscar Wright	Virginia	Virginia	Virginia									
Mattie Wright	Virginia	Virginia	Virginia									
Allomillia Wright	Virginia	Virginia	Virginia									
Ben Wright	Virginia	Virginia	Virginia									
Hattie Wright	Virginia	Virginia	Virginia									

June 9 1900

Randal Bryant	Virginia	Virginia	Virginia				OT(?)		.	no	no	yes
Julia A Bryant	Virginia	Virginia	Virginia						.	no	no	yes
India Wright	Virginia	Virginia	Virginia						.	no	no	yes
Mattie Brown	Virginia	Virginia	Virginia						5	yes	yes	yes
Maud Agee	Virginia	Virginia	Virginia						5	yes	yes	yes
London Wright	Virginia	Virginia	Virginia						5	yes	no	yes
Ernest Wright	Virginia	Virginia	Virginia						.	no	no	yes
Eddie Wilkinson	Virginia	Virginia	Virginia						.	yes	yes	yes

Appendix: Cumberland County, Virginia, 1900 Census

Name of each person whose place of abode on June 1, 1900, was in this family. [continued from prior page]	Ownership Of Home				Identification
	Owned or rented	Owned free or mortgaged	Farm or house	Number of farm schedule	

June 7, 1900

George Wright	R		F	6	1940 George Bently or Bent Wright of Cumberland County, son of 1863 William
Pattie Wright					Wright of Buckingham County, probably grandson of 1803 John Wright of
William Wright					Cumberland County, great grandson of 1770 John Wright of Cumberland
Emeline Wright					Coiunty, and great great grandson of 1769 George Wright of Essex County
Oscar Wright					
Mattie Wright					
Allomillia Wright					
Ben Wright					
Hattie Wright					

June 9 1900

Randal Bryant	R		H		
Julia A Bryatn					
India Wright					
Mattie Brown					
Maud Agee					
London Wright					
Ernest Wright					
Eddie Wilkinson					

Appendix: Cumberland County, Virginia, 1900 Census

Location				Relation	Personal Description							
In Cities		Number of dwelling houses in the order of visitation	Number of family in the order of visitation	Name of each person whose place of abode on June 1, 1900, was in this family.	Relationship of each person to the head the family	Color or race	Sex	Date of Birth		Age at last birthday	Whether single, married, widowed, or divorced	Number of years married	Mother of how many children	Number of these children living
Street	House Number							Month	Year					

June 25, 1900

		209	212	Lafayette C Wright	Head	W	M	April	1855	45	M	25	.	.
				Sarah S Wright	Wife	W	F	May	1847	53	M	25	5	3
				William F Wright	Son	W	M	May	1875	25	M	4	.	.
				Rosa L Wright	Dr in Law	W	F	May	1872	27	M	4	3	3
				Walter E Wright	Son	W	M	April	1883	17	S	.	.	.
				Lizzie F Wright	Daughter	W	F	June	1889	10	S	.	.	.
				Horace F Wright	Gr Son	W	M	Dec	1897	2	S	.	.	.
				Gertrude L Wright	Gr Daughter	W	F	Nov	1898	1	S	.	.	.
				Mollie E Wright	Gr Daughter	W	F	Nov	1899	6/12	S	.	.	.

June 29, 1900

		237	241	Jonas Wright	Heade	W	M	July	1864	35	M	15	.	.
				Mattie Wright	wife	W	F	Feb	1872	28	M	15	4	4
				Robert Wright	Son	W	M	May	1887	13	S	.	.	.
				Frank Wright	Son	W	M	Mar	1893	7	S	.	.	.
				Martha L Wright	Daughter	W	F	April	1897	3	S	.	.	.

Appendix: Cumberland County, Virginia, 1900 Census

Name of each person whose place of abode on June 1, 1900, was in this family. [continued from prior page]	Nativity			Citizenship			Occupation, Trade, Or Profession of each person Ten Years of age and over.		Education			
	Place of birth of each person and parents of each person enumerated											
	Place of birth of this Person	Place of birth of Father of this person	Place of birth of Mother of this person	Year of immigration to the United States	Number of years in the United States	Natural- ization	Occupation	Months not employed	Attended school in months)	Can read	Can write	Can speak English

June 9, 1900

Lafayette C Wright	Virginia	Virginia	Virginia				Farmer	0	.	Yes	Yes	Yes
Sarah S Wright	Virginia	Virginia	Virginia				..	.	.	Yes	Yes	Yes
William F Wright	Virginia	Virginia	Virginia				Farm Laborer	0	.	Yes	Yes	Yes
Rosa L Wright	Virginia	Virginia	Virginia				.	.	.	Yes	Yes	Yes
Walter E Wright	Virginia	Virginia	Virginia				Farm Laborer	0	.	Yes	Yes	Yes
Lizzie F Wright	Virginia	Virginia	Virginia				At School	.	5	Yes	Yes	Yes
Horace F Wright	Virginia	Virginia	Virginia				.	.	.	.	.	.
Gertrude L Wright	Virginia	Virginia	Virginia				.	.	.	.	.	.
Mollie E Wright	Virginia	Virginia	Virginia				.	.	.	.	.	.
Mary Wright	Virginia	Virginia	Virginia				.	.	.	.	.	.

June 29, 1900

Jonas Wright	Virginia	Virginia	Virginia				Farmer	0		yes	yes	yes
Mattie Wright	Virginia	Virginia	Virginia				.	.		yes	yes	yes
Robert Wright	Virginia	Virginia	Virginia				Farm laborer	0		yes	yes	yes
Frank Wright	Virginia	Virginia	Virginia				.	.		.	.	.
Martha L Wright	Virginia	Virginia	Virginia				.	.		.	.	.

Appendix: Cumberland County, Virginia, 1900 Census

Name of each person whose place of abode on June 1, 1900, was in this family. [continued from prior page]	Ownership Of Home				Identification
	Owned or rented	Owned free or mortgaged	Farm or house	Number of farm schedule	

June 9, 1900

Lafayette C Wright	R		F	190	Lafayette Clifton Wright, son of 1910 William P. Wright of Prince Edward County, grandson of Daniel P. Wright, great grandson of 1811 John Wright of Campbell County, and great great grandson of Robert Wright, Sr. (Campbell County)
Sarah S Wright					
William F Wright					
Rosa L Wright					
Walter E Wright					
Lizzie F Wright					
Horace F Wright					
Gertrude L Wright					
Mollie E Wright					
Mary Wright					

June 29, 1900

Jonas Wright	R	F	F	195	1940 Jonas Manville Wright of Cumberland County, son of 1905 James A. Wright of Buckingham County, grandson of 1863 William Wright of Buckingham County, probably great grandson of 1803 John Wright of Cumberland County, great great grandson of 1770 John Wright of Cumberland County, and great great great grandson of 1769 George Wright of Essex County
Mattie Wright					
Robert Wright					
Frank Wright					
Martha L Wright					

INDEX

Agee, Maud, 38, 39, 40
Anderson, Susan, 24
Anderson, William B, 24
Ayres, John G., 28, 29
Brown, Mattie, 38, 39, 40
Bryant, Julia A, 38, 39
Bryant, Randal, 38, 39, 40
Bryatn, Julia A, 40
Bundrant, Maria, 33, 34
Dowdy, N. A., 28, 29
Goodman, Burley, 28, 29
Goodman, Frances, 28, 29
Goodman, Frances W, 33, 34
Goodman, Henry, 28, 29
Goodman, Lilia, 28, 29
Goodman, Molly, 28, 29
Goodman, Robert, 28, 29
Goodman, Robt J, 33, 34
Gray, Davie, 33, 34
Gray, Martha, 33, 34
Gray, Sam, 33, 34
Meador, Julia, 28, 29
Meador, Louise, 28, 29
Meador, Michael, 28, 29
Palmore, John R., 28, 29
Right, Green, 2
Right, Seaymore, 2, 3
Right, William, 2, 3
Right jr, Seaymore, 2, 3
Sales, Cornelius, 33, 34
Smith, Billy, 26
Wilkinson, Eddie, 38, 39, 40
Wright, Agnes, 30,31
Wright, Allomillia, 38, 39, 40
Wright, Ann, 24, 28, 29, 33, 34
Wright, Ann A, 24
Wright, Ben, 38, 39, 40

Wright, Cary, 35, 36
Wright, Catharine, 26
Wright, Charles, 24
Wright, Edmond, 35, 36
Wright, Edmund, 28, 29
Wright, Edward F, 26
Wright, Elizabeth, 16, 17, 18, 19, 20, 21, 22
Wright, Emeline, 38, 39, 40
Wright, Ernest, 38, 39, 40
Wright, Frank, 41, 42, 43
Wright, Geoge, 33, 34
Wright, George, 28, 29, 38, 39, 40
Wright, Gertrude L, 41, 42, 43
Wright, Green, 3
Wright, Hal, 28
Wright, Hal, 29
Wright, Hattie, 38, 39, 40
Wright, Horace F, 41, 42, 43
Wright, India, 38, 39,4 0
Wright, Ivanna F., 24
Wright, James, 24
Wright, James A., 26
Wright, John, 28, 29
Wright, John S, 26
Wright, John W, 9, 10, 11, 12, 13, 14, 16, 17, 18, 19, 20, 21, 22, 24
Wright, Jonas, 41, 42, 43
Wright, Lafayette C, 41, 42, 43
Wright, Lizzie F, 41, 42, 43
Wright, London, 38, 39, 40
Wright, Louisa, 30, 31
Wright, Margaret D, 24
Wright, Martha, 35, 36
Wright, Martha L, 41, 42, 43
Wright, Mary, 30, 31, 42, 43
Wright, Mary E, 24
Wright, Mattie, 38, 39, 40, 41, 42, 43

Wright, Mollie E, 41, 42, 43
Wright, Nancy, 24, 28, 29
Wright, Nathaniel, 24
Wright, Nina L, 24
Wright, Oscar, 38, 39, 40
Wright, Pattie, 33, 34, 38, 39, 40
Wright, Philip, 26
Wright, Philip W, 9, 10, 11, 12, 13, 14
Wright, Pleasant, 9, 10, 11, 12, 13, 14, 16, 17, 18, 19, 20, 21, 22
Wright, Robert, 41, 432, 43
Wright, Rosa L, 41, 42, 43
Wright, Samuel, 9, 10, 11, 12, 13, 14
Wright, Sarah, 26
Wright, Sarah E, 24
Wright, Sarah S, 41, 42, 43
Wright, Semere, 26
Wright, Seymore, 5, 6, 7
Wright, Simon, 28, 29, 33, 34
Wright, Sophie, 28, 29, 30, 31
Wright, Thomas, 24
Wright, Thomas H, 26
Wright, Walter E, 41, 42, 43
Wright, William, 5, 6, 7, 9, 10, 11, 12, 13, 14, 33, 34, 38, 39, 40
Wright, William F, 41, 42, 43
Wright, William R, 9, 10, 11, 12, 13, 14
Wright, William S., 26
Wright, Wyatt, 30, 31

0391(122113)

Heritage Books by Robert N. Grant

Lynchburg

Wright Family Records: Lynchburg, Virginia Birth Records (1853–1896), Marriage Records (1805–1900), Marriage Notices (1794–1880), Census Records (1900), Deed Records (1805–1900), Death Records (1853–1896), Probate Records (1805–1900)

Amherst County

Wright Family Birth Records, 1853–1896; Marriage Records, 1761–1900; Census Records, 1810–1900, in Amherst County, Virginia

Wright Family Land Tax Records: Amherst County, Virginia, 1782–1850

Wright Family Patent Deeds and Land Grants, 1761–1900, Deed Records, 1761–1903; Chancery Court Files, 1804–1900; Death Records, 1853–1920; Cemetery Records by Cemetery; and Probate Records, 1761–1900, in Amherst County, Virginia

Wright Family Personal Property Tax Lists: Amherst County, Virginia, 1782–1850

Appomattox County

Wright Family Birth Records, Marriage Records, and Personal Property Tax Lists: Appomattox County, Virginia

Wright Family Census Records, Deed Records, Land Tax Lists, Death Records and Probate Records: Appomattox County, Virginia

Bedford County

Wright Family Census Records: Bedford County, Virginia, 1810–1900

Wright Family Death, Cemetery and Probate Records: Bedford County, Virginia

Wright Family Land Records: Bedford County, Virginia

Wright Family Personal Property Tax Records for Bedford County, Virginia, 1782 to 1850

Wright Family Records: Births in Bedford County, Virginia

Wright Family Records: Land Tax List, Bedford County, Virginia, 1782–1850

Wright Family Records: Marriages in Bedford County, Virginia

Campbell County

Wright Family Birth Records (1853–1896) and Marriage Records (1782–1900): Campbell County, Virginia

Wright Family Census Records: Campbell County, Virginia, 1810–1900

Wright Family Death Records (1853–1920), Cemetery Records by Cemetery, and Probate Records (1782–1900): Campbell County, Virginia

Wright Family Deed Records (1782–1900) and Land Tax List (1782–1850): Campbell County, Virginia

Wright Family Personal Property Tax Lists: Campbell County, Virginia, 1785–1850

Cumberland County

Wright Family Birth, Marriage, Personal Property Tax and Census Records, Cumberland County, Virginia

Wright Family Deed, Land Tax, Death and Probate Records, Cumberland County, Virginia

Essex County

Wright Family Birth, Marriage, and Personal Property Tax Records, Essex County, Virginia

Wright Family Census, Deed, Land Tax, Death and Probate Records, Essex County, Virginia

Fauquier County

The Identification of 1792 John Wright of Fauquier County, Virginia, as Not the Son of 1792/30 John Wright of Stafford County, Virginia

Franklin County

The Identification of 1809 William Wright of Franklin County, Virginia, as the Son of 1792 John Wright of Fauquier County, Virginia, and Elizabeth (Bronaugh) (Darnall) Wright

Wright Family Birth Records (1853–1896) and Marriage Records (1788–1915): Franklin County, Virginia, 1853–1896

Wright Family Census Records: Franklin County, Virginia, 1810–1900

Wright Family Death Records (1854–1920), Cemetery Records by Cemetery, and Probate Records (1785–1928): Franklin County, Virginia

Wright Family Land Grants (1785–1900) and Deed Records (1785–1897): Franklin County, Virginia

Wright Family Land Tax Lists: Franklin County, Virginia, 1786–1860

Wright Family Personal Property Tax Lists: Franklin County, Virginia, 1786–1850

Goochland County

Identifying the Wrights in the Goochland County, Virginia Tithe Lists, 1732–84

Montgomery County

Wright Family Birth, Marriage, and Personal Property Tax Records, Montgomery County, Virginia

Wright Family Census, Land Grants, Land Tax, Deed, Death, and Probate Records, Montgomery County, Virginia

Nelson County

Wright Family Birth Records, 1853–1896; Marriage Records, 1808–1910; Census Records, 1810–1900; Patent Deeds and Land Grants; Deed Records, 1808–1910; Death Records, 1853–1896; Probate Records, 1808–1900, in Nelson County, Virginia

Wright Family Land Tax Records: Nelson County, Virginia, 1809–1850

Wright Family Personal Property Tax Lists: Nelson County, Virginia, 1809–1850

Prince Edward County

Wright Family Land Grants, Deed Records, Land Tax List, Death Records, Probate Records: Prince Edward County, Virginia

Wright Family Records: Prince Edward County, Virginia Birth Records, Marriage Records, Election Polls, and Tithe List, Personal Property Tax List, Census

Rockbridge County

Wright Family Birth Records, 1853–1896; Marriage Records, 1777–1918; Census Records, 1810–1900; Deed Records, 1777–1902; Death Records, 1853–1896; Cemetery Records, and Probate Records, 1777–1909; in Rockbridge County, Virginia

Wright Family Land Tax Lists: Rockbridge County, Virginia, 1782–1850

Wright Family Personal Property Tax Lists: Rockbridge County, Virginia, 1782–1850

www.ingramcontent.com/pod-product-compliance
Lightning Source LLC
Chambersburg PA
CBHW081126170426
43197CB00017B/2766